AGENDA

Keenings

AGENDA

CONTENTS

Editorial and Introduction		6
INTERVIEW and POEMS		
Peter Dale		8
POEMS		
Mary Fitzpatrick:	Our Fortune's Made Up of Our Friends The Empty Bed Sheets May Altar The Mole	28
Robin Houghton:	River Ouse, Rodmell, 1941	32
John Griffin:	Wonderland The Waves	33
Marek Urbanowicz:	Mr. Audley's Daughter	37
Gill McEvoy:	Laying the White Rose Conservatory	39
Kevin Cahill:	Peaseblossom Reconciliation	41
Chris Fletcher:	125mph Keys	43
Warren Stutely:	ars nova song coast	45
Eleanor Hooker:	54 Recovery Songs of the Sea	47

Robert Smith:	Aphasia Telephone	50
Stuart Medland:	One Moment Fingerprints Ford Toughening Up	51
Alfonso Reyes:	Farewell Ballad of the Dead Friends *Translated by Timothy Adès*	59
Avril Staple:	If You Hadn't Died So Young	62
Maureen Duffy:	The Book of the Dead	63

ESSAYS/REVIEWS

James Aitchison:	Chain of Being: The Fellowship of Dead Poets	64
Patricia McCarthy:	Talking to the Dead: R.V. Bailey's *The Losing Game* Penelope Shuttle's *Sandgrain and Hourglass* Tim Liardet's *The Storm House* Gjertrud Schnackenberg's *Heavenly Questions*	71

POEMS

Lyn Moir:	Guggenheim Swans Train from Aranjuéz	84
M.H. Miles:	August Chain Mail The Flats	86
Abegail Morley:	Place	88
Nigel Holt:	Eldorado	89
D.W. Brydon:	Shells	91

James Roberts:	The Graveyard of Little St. David's	92
Tim Murdoch:	The Ancestral Imperative Green Man Blues	93
Peter Rawlings:	Living in the Dark The Apple Room	95
Sarah Ruden:	King David Refuses to Mourn His Son	98
Sue Roe:	Her Little Gloves	99
Jackie Wills:	Woman's legs as path Woman's head as jug	100
Don Avery:	The Egg Room	101
William Francis:	'Would you like to see her?'	102
Dylan Willoughby:	Annwn	103
Charles Baudelaire:	I Give You These Lines Meditation *Translated by Jan Owen*	104
Sergey Pantsirev:	All Said *Translated by Richard McKane*	106
Roald Mandelstam:	Dance of Shades *Translated by Richard McKane*	107

ESSAYS/REVIEWS

W. S. Milne:	'Unknown modes of being': Geoffrey Hill's Late Poetry: Geoffrey Hill's *Oraclau* Geoffrey Hill's *Clavics*	108

Josephine Balmer:	A Day in the Life: Michael Longley's *A Hundred Doors* Brendan Kennelly: *The Essential Brendan Kennelly: Selected Poems* Derek Mahon: *New Collected Poems*	117
William Bedford:	Exiles: David Harsent's *Night* Bernard O'Donoghue's *Farmers Cross* John Montague's *Speech Lessons* Christine O'Neill's *The Scent Gallery* David Cooke's *In the Distance*	123
Belinda Cooke:	Snicking at Edges Gill McEvoy: *The Plucking Shed* Jean O'Brien: *Lovely Legs* Louise C. Callaghan: *In the Ninth House* Matthew Barton: *Vessel* Tony Roberts: *Outsiders*	130

NOTES FOR BROADSHEET POETS: 142

Agenda Poetry Competition
Results and comments

BIOGRAPHIES 156

Front cover painting: *Small Deathbed Scene* by **Max Beckmann**
© bpk / Nationalgalerie, SMB / Jörg P. Anders

Editorial and Introduction

Important news: *Agenda*'s archive and its website are being preserved in The Bodleian Library, Oxford. So all the poets, essayists and artists who have appeared and will appear in *Agenda* and on its website – and all the readers and subscribers who give their breath to *Agenda*'s pages – will have an honourable place for perpetuity in The Bodleian.

Because of the results of *Agenda*'s first poetry competition and the comments on it, it has been decided just this once not to include any chosen young Broadsheet poets in this issue. All young Broadsheet poets will feature in the online Broadsheet 17, along with the work of young artists. Do visit www.agendapoetry.co.uk for this and also for the online web supplement (of poems and paintings) to this issue. Included will be a chosen clutch of poems sent in to the competition.

*

Welcome to this 'Keenings' issue of Agenda through which runs an echo from a refrain of an old Irish keening or caoineadh: 'Ochón agus ochón ó'. The assonance of the 'o' gives meaning to the sound of the lament which does not even need to be understood.

The whole subject of death is inclined to be a sanitised taboo in our society with heavy wooden coffins (thank goodness for the more recent wicker ones). This is unlike in Ireland, and indeed in the Indian continent, for example, where at Pashupatinath temple in Kathmandhu I remember death being folded into life, corpses stuffed with straw taken to the Holy River, wrapped in white shrouds. There, the legs of the lepers one side of a stone ghat, and those of the more wealthy the other side, were trailed in the brown current, their souls being washed downstream for reincarnation in another existence. Then the body of the deceased loved one was set alight while children chanted and skipped around it.

Poetry has always managed to deal with the difficult, and it is this issue of *Agenda*, woven around the theme of elegies, that words do come into their own and prove that this is so. The poems here surely comply with what Elizabeth Jennings, in *Every Changing Shape*, wrote about Rilke's elegies: 'the tension in these great elegies lies in the implicit yet unacknowledged belief that reality exists autonomously in an area of experience that only poetry can penetrate'.

To get into the mood for this 'Keenings' issue, then, let us listen to Galway Kinnell: '...poetry sings past even the sadness / that begins it' and 'When the song goes, silence replaces it / inside the bones'.

Inspiring ideas for early Christmas presents

Three special new collections from AGENDA Editions

James Simpson - *The Untenanted Room* (£10)

Woodcuts by Carolyn Trant

The Untenanted Room, with its elusive and haunting power, is unlike anything else I know of since Eliot and Hughes. It holds together a mythic personal narrative with the desolate gravity of our present general condition, in vigorous contemporary language which draws strength from its ancient roots and its kinship with the natural world, which we despoil even as it sustains us.

Lindsay Clarke

It is an impressive work, deeply serious, ambitious, and powerful. It addresses important issues; indeed, the 'place' where we are: 'that place/not properly inhabited,/swept clean, adrift, cut off,/hung on the grid of numbers'. Its language has a strong Anglo-Saxon feel, which corresponds to a feeling for earth, landscape, and the relation between language and the organic and animal creation.

Jeremy Hooker

Andrew McNeillie – Losers Keepers (£9)

> By day the draft under the door
> and a deep window's long skies
> turned his head from print to thought
> and what precedes them both.

'No halfers . . .' one version has it, 'losers weepers, finders keepers.' But Andrew McNeillie in these poems has halved things to make a paradox. 'Finders keepers' reminds him too much of the rough justice of schoolboys and emperors. 'Losers weepers' on the other hand he considers altogether too melancholy. 'Losers keepers' offers a way through, and as Robert Frost said, 'The best way out is always through.'

We live in and through our losses day by day. At the time they may seem like gains. But they are all fleeting. We keep a hold on what we can of them. This is the work attempted by these poems, chiefly in two territories, in Ireland and Scotland, with a triangulation to 'the ancient shades, the ghosts of youth' in Oxford. Somewhat in the spirit of latter-day lyrical ballads, they include elegies or memorials to both obscure lives and more prominent ones, and lyrics that speak from the extremities of living memory.

Both the above books can be ordered from: Agenda, The Wheelwrights, Fletching Street, Mayfield, East Sussex TN20 6TL or telephone 01435 873703. Visa and MasterCard accepted. Cheques payable to *Agenda*.

Arthur Terry: A Woman Called Rose (£9)

Translated from the Spanish of Angel Crespo

An inspired, beautifully-crafted collection of big, moving poems from this master-translator and Catalan scholar.

Seamus Heaney refers to the 'delicate iambic cadences of Arthur Terry's translations'. These are evidenced here, along with his stress on intonation, that 'living part of a poem' – as Robert Frost said – which is 'entangled somehow in the syntax idiom and meaning of a sentence'.

INTERVIEW
Peter Dale

Patricia McCarthy: With your imminent *Diffractions: New and Collected Poems* coming out from Anvil, it seems fitting to interview you here, Peter, about your impressive and important corpus of poetry. Also about its nurturing, in the early days of *Agenda*, by William Cookson, the magazine's founding and longstanding editor. He said, on first discovering your poetry, 'I was struck immediately that here was the true voice of feeling' and he went on to praise your special 'electric energy – the only touchstone on which I can rely'. The only touchstone on which *Agenda* still relies, rare as it may be. As a man in your early seventies now, if it is not unfair to ask you, what would you say about your own passionate work – when you view it retrospectively?

Peter Dale: All I can suggest is that, when you're young and obsessively committed as William and I were at that heady outset, as poets you have some probably over directional ideas as to where and how you want your poems to go. As editors we perhaps sometimes had too much idea as to where we wanted other people's poems to go. As your work develops with experience and knowledge and – shall we say marks out its own itinerary? – all that certainty modifies. Years later, when you look back over your route you're often surprised, even shocked, not always unpleasantly, at where it has taken you and what turned out to be the turns and fingerposts along it. You can't predict or hope in your twenties that lines jotted down at fifteen will resurface in a book of your seventies. But that is the sort of surprise that happens. Laforgue, I think, said a poem should surprise the author. I suppose the whole writing life also does that in several respects. Yet, through all the varied poems and methods adopted and running through the books, one still feels a consistent current or vein of ore underlying it from that original compulsion to write poems. That commitment and drive survives and is even deepened.

PMcC: In the Peter Dale Fiftieth Birthday issue of *Agenda*, it is said that, like Yeats, you just get better and better. However, I would posit that your sonnet sequence, *One Another*, written when you were a young man, cannot be bettered. And immediately belongs to the canon of the greatest literature. As William Cookson (who died in January 2003) says of your work in general, it has the rare quality of 'pure emotion'. Had you only written that one sequence in your life, it would have been a complete achievement.

PD: It's good of you to suggest such an achievement – and gratifying. Most poets do improve, though the writing trajectory of most of us is a parabola.

I'm not sure about *pure* emotion, a difficult idea. Most emotions are mixed and seem more so as you grow older. That is one area that more and more often surfaced in the poems. I think the work has expanded much beyond *One Another*. The best is often the hindrance to the better – or creatively different. *Local Habitation* and, on a miniature scale, *Da Capo,* both of which emerge from some of *One Another*'s concerns, would run it pretty close if not overtake it in many respects, though poets do tend to prefer their recent work, for a year or two at least. *Like a Vow* also takes off on a different tangent, formally and thematically.

(What ought to bother me more than it does, if your remarks are anywhere near right, is how little notice *One Another* has received over the years. Incidentally, as well as that sequence, I've written quite a few other sonnets, *Mirrors, Windows* is another short sequence for example, but none of my sonnets, to my knowledge, appear in recent anthologies of sonnets and sonnet forms.)

PMcC: The first person singular that you use in *One Another* is the creative 'I' of poetic imagination, and presumably accounts for the 'anonymity' you claim behind all your personae. Do you, then, not distinguish this anonymous 'I' from the personal 'I' which must occasionally be there in your poems e.g. those to your father?

PD: The answer is probably best given by a pair of odd-fellow poets. To misappropriate Rimbaud slightly, 'Je est un autre.' Or Emily Dickinson who said, 'When I state myself, as the Representative of the Verse – it does not mean – me – but a supposed Person.' She also wrote in a letter that the ideal reader is someone 'who permits a comfortable intimacy and yet lets the innermost Me remain behind its veil.' Those early poems were constructed out of those paternal religious pressures pounding against my temperament, reading, education, and growing literary commitment. The actual details they appear to record were imaginatively invented in an attempt at exorcism or excision. My father died when I was away at college – which was the final brutal excision. After that the poems changed. The issue was not so much my father as religion. The personal pronouns are dramatic characters, not so much biographical ones. To develop an image from Mallarmé, if I remember right: assume life is a stained glass window, made of experience, encounters, incidents. What the arts do is to break it into fragments and put those pieces into a kaleidoscope in which the artist finds changing patterns of, shall we say, vicarious reality. The shaking is sometimes a nervous twitch, a jolt of discovery, or sometimes a tremor of shock or terror.

PMcC: An interesting idea: the personal pronouns being the dramatic characters. A form of allegory, I suppose.

PD: No allegories, I think. If writers cannot imagine and record another character or two, it's a hopeless look-out for literature, and life in general, I think. Are we all falling into autistic misfunction? Social intercourse would be even more difficult than it is if we couldn't put ourselves into someone else's shoes, imagine other minds. The 'I' and the 'you' in the various poems represent a collection of different imagined characters at salient moments or significant junctures. To have employed proper names in poems would start all sorts of hunts for identities that don't exist in flesh and blood. (See the comment on *Local Habitation* later.)

PMcC: Could the fabled woman of these wonderfully achieved, passionate sonnets in *One Another* be your anima, your muse? Linking in with this, it is interesting that you mention somewhere that women's voices, disembodied, often come to you, even in dreams or after sleep. These are not, I notice, always soft, gentle voices – perhaps reminiscent of the mother you lost so early – but harsh, even aggressive at times, coming, maybe from a dark or shadow side of your subconscious self.

PD: I'm no Gravesian muse poet: 'I came to the garden of Love / And found it was fillèd with Graves.' The muse is no more than a useful metaphor for the weird things that imaginative and artistic people experience. Poems in all sorts of voices and on all sorts of topics are experiences made of words and words have voices, speech and rhythms of their own. (There are eidetic voices, I'm told, as well as visual images like Macbeth's dagger. He too heard voices.) Yet you are right about what I would call the feistiness of these female voices. ('A Woman Speaks to God the Father' is a good example.) The voices seem to exercise an interest in science over the romanticism of the male voices. So it is a sort of reverse of roles as they were once stereotyped. The self is a river. It can never be still. The same is true of the flow of poems. This is why I said earlier that one is surprised at the course the work has taken and what turned out to be the signposts along it. It's only when looking back over things that I noticed this feisty and scientific turn of mind in the female voices. But there's a lot of culinary imagery in the speech of Gill in *Local Habitation*. That, too, surprised me.

My mother died when I was nearly a teenager but I suspect in hindsight the abrasiveness of the imagined voices, the sardonic, ironic humour and earthiness may come from her side of the family.

P McC: You did say to me, when your latest collection *Local Habitation* came out from Anvil (2009), that you believed it to be your best book. I find it very interesting a development as it uses three voices in an original way dramatically and mixes very well the lyric with narrative, along with touches of imagism. Midway between verse drama and a poetry sequence, it is also perhaps more inaccessible, particularly in terms of narrative, than your earlier work. Can you comment on this book? And on any residual influences of modernism on you?

PD: The book came as a complete surprise to me. In fact, it intervened in the middle of another collection I was making. This collection would not gel and was driving me crazy. You may remember we both looked at what is now the opening poem of *Local Habitation* at the Ledbury festival, after William's death, and we'd discussed its dialogue structure. Well, later, that idea suddenly took life of its own and started landing poems like patterns of starlings coming in to roost. One of the few creative bonuses of the computer is that you can easily apply different fonts to words and that, in itself, made for a compositional – in both senses – excitement. The book gave Peter Jay a great deal of trouble and hard work to set. We spent a whole day trying to find three type-faces that would be distinct for the reader yet blend well enough not to be a typographical mess. We could not do it. In the end, we came up with the current system. It seems to work well and is not obtrusive. Not all of the remembrances and slips of memory are indicated, anyway, because in life we are not always aware of such verbal echoes of ourselves or other people. Oddly the character names derive from typeface names: *Joanna, Gill Sans* and *Dan*te – a residue of the typographical beginnings.

Curiously, after the first *Mortal Fire* from Macmillan in 1970, I had said to myself: you can't write this poem properly until you're old. I didn't know it would eventually turn into the concerns and shapes it made in *Local Habitation*. As for any residual influences of modernism, yes, I suppose there may be some of these in the sequences after *One Another*. Modernism, in its American form, asked a great deal of the reader, often too much and too subjectively. But some readers have said that I expect too much of them, too much mental agility. All I can say is that if so, none of it was deliberate. You have to distinguish, as Coleridge pointed out, between the expression of obscurity and obscurity of expression. The modernists did not always do that. Yet I think it was Collingwood who remarked that if you aim to make a foolproof book you are choosing fools for your readers. And, if I remember right, it was Auden who did remark that, when a fool told him how much he admired his poems, he felt as if he had picked his pocket. You want to write poems that people grow into and, with luck, grow with. Good work, literature, is meant to receive more than just one reading. It's not discardable holiday reading.

PMcC: As this issue of *Agenda* focuses on elegies, can you enlarge upon the elegiac content of *Local Habitation*. And indeed on the elegiac running through your work, including in the very fine *Da Capo* sequence, with its two voices, you sent me before it was published.

PD: Yes, looking back, I was surprised to find how often I was drawn to the elegiac. It's partly the effect of surviving friends and family but it goes a bit further back than that, to a war-time childhood, the early death of mother and later of father, and working in hospital. The dedication to *Local Habitation*, in memoriam to my younger brother and his first two children, marks another elegiac recognition of what Delmore Schwartz called 'the heavy bear that goes with me, meaning death.'

PMcC: Apart from mourning humans, you also mourn memory itself, dreams – 'if the dreams came they would weep', and words or language such as the secret names and even the 'nameless anonymity' behind names. 'The fonts outlast the names that we bestow', you claim. Is this connected to your being a materialist, influenced by Ayer?

PD: Don't forget 'fonts' represents two things: the baptismal and the printed, the living and the recorded. The second sort gets rearranged in monotype; electronic words are even more ephemeral. We speak of living memory but when you go and look at an old memorial stone or column you find names there of no one known to you. They aren't really names any more beyond that. They are dead memory. It's a terrible but abiding thought. It's not a direct consequence of materialism to feel this. *Sic transit gloria mundi.* 'Memory fades / Must the remembered perishing be?' The placing of 'perishing' is powerful. The awareness of transitoriness and mutability was around long before scientific materialism took off. Even the churches of the resurrection are filled with carved memorials of the once consequent and well-to-do dead and the buildings are surrounded by graves. That always strikes me as ironic and contradictory. Peter Levi, poet and ex-priest, wrote: 'All the consolations are false.'

PMcC: William Bedford, in the Peter Dale Fiftieth Anniversary issue of *Agenda*, talks of the 'tension between narrative and epiphany' in your work. The fact that epiphanies do proliferate might suggest a contradiction to your materialist views.

PD: I don't agree with that. Epiphanies, I think, don't *proliferate*. I rather dislike the term 'epiphany' with its religious origins. Let's just say there are a few good and lively moments or poems, like pylons holding up the power lines. They don't contradict materialism. In fact, they may indirectly highlight it and the transitoriness of even stars, galaxies. Most of life is a set of punctuating high-lit or gilded beads sliding along a string of rather dull and repeating actualities.

PMcC: I felt at times, in *Local Habitation*, though your own voice is highly distinctive, an influence of the Medieval Miracle & Mystery Plays in the tone you frequently employ, also of Geoffrey Hill in condensed, beautiful but not immediately accessible passages. Were you aware of these influences? Or perhaps of others such as Hardy and Blake who also come to mind and echo in your work in general?

PD: The poets you mention, not the plays, have frequently impressed me but it's other people's job to worry about influences – like twitchers scurrying after rare birds. I like Hill's idea of the lyric as a stage on which a drama occurs: he said, 'lyric poetry is necessarily dramatic ...' There's the embodied drama of ideas there, too. Mischievously, I think there's a slight influence of Ursula le Guin in some poems but it wouldn't be pellucidly clear for most critics or readers and might now start a few hares. (Detection of influence seems often to depend on what the detective has recently been reading.)

PMcC: Do you see your whole oeuvre as a single continuum, irrespective of chronological details?

PD: No. It just exists in a time-space continuum. As Larkin remarked you don't write what you please; you write what you can. Writing is a compulsion; you write what insists on being written. In a sense that fact absorbed Valéry; he suggested poems write you. You don't know what the poem is until it turns up finished. If there's a continuum you don't have much choice of what sort it is. Speaking for myself, I don't think you can consciously plan or make synopses for future poems, Some poems intrude that you actually don't want to write but, in the end, you have to do them to regain your equilibrium until next time. A lyric poet's continuum is just one damn thing after another. Looking back, I suppose the only strand that might suggest a continuum is the theme of people and the complications of communication in human relationships with imagery of the external world as the linking contextualisation. But the poems seem to come in chunks: the narrative diversion, the move into duologue methods, from *One Another* till

Local Habitation, a period interleaved with most of the translations and verse drama. Now it seems to be elegies, epigrams and song – among them carol texts wanted by composer friends.

I don't intend to suggest that poems bypass the brain in some inspirational way. Once the nub of a poem arrives it comes under the gentle irremissive power of the understanding and the will, as Coleridge said. As for chronology, how is a poem dated: from first inkling, first draft or final revision? Some poems, even short ones, may take years before they're finally achieved.

P McC: For many years you were *Agenda*'s life-blood and pulse – as co-editor with the founding editor, William Cookson, your peer in your student days at Oxford. You were also very good friends with Ian Hamilton. Did you find your studies conducive to, and encouraging of, your poetry? Or was it the intensity of these two friendships and the sense, always, of being an outsider, that launched you on the poet's perilous, obsessive path?

PD: Not an outsider; just no good as a team-player. William was the life-blood of *Agenda*. Pound was often a virus in his system. I may have been its alternative therapy consultant of dubious effect.

I knew I was going to be a poet from the age of fourteen. This drive became more compulsive as I grew up and meeting other poets confirmed it. College vacations spent in Oxford gave me plenty of time to write and think about writing and to discuss it. I've said elsewhere how useless the tutoring and lectures seemed to be then. I remember remarking to Ian once, long after our college discussions, that I sometimes wished I'd never been a poet and supposed he felt the same. He replied by asking what option we had. We both agreed; none at all. (Send for the shrinks.) The three of us were in the same bind.

Another poet was a vital friend to me then. Kevin Crossley-Holland was the first student I met at college who was a committed poet and on a shared wave-length. He was my first publisher up until he got Penguin to take my Villon. We were perhaps more in sympathy in the spectrum of feeling in Anglo-Saxon verse. He later translated *Beowulf* and the old English poems. I used his *Beowulf* for years in teaching.

As for our studies, prescribed, book-based education can also often hinder a writer more than help. It can make you see things with ideas thicker than frosted glasses over your eyes. It can make the intelligence more dominating than STC's gentle irremissive power. I had to shake that off or, at least dilute it, and trust the poem in its inception and development. I do things in verse with equanimity now that might well have appalled my younger intelligence.

PMcC: I remember your helpful handwritten comments on some of my poems that I sent to you from Bangladesh and Nepal where I was living at that time as a young woman. And your kind of adoption of me as an *Agenda* poet, after which we used to swap poems for quite a few years, giving feedback to each other. Did you find it rewarding being a mentor in general? And did you find editing/using your critical powers, like teaching, the best way of learning or evolving?

PD: I'm glad I was some use but, looking back, I think poet-editors can hinder as well as help. Kipling said that there are a hundred and sixty-nine ways of writing tribal lays and that every one of them was right. I would not have believed a number anywhere near that in my twenties but he makes a point. We had quite detailed discussions and continuing arguments, Ian, William, Kevin and I over our poems, each staring through his own critical eye-piece. Not one of us then wanted to give an inch. It was a bit of luck that we weren't too divergent from, or antagonistic to, one another's approach.

It was the same with your poems, if I remember right. Poets have their proclivities and obsessions to protect.

Yet the printing of verse was always vastly wider than the production of real poems. The proportion of the first expanded, once printing came in. Now electronic means have merely increased the production of all sorts of verse and worse while removing most of the critical filters and, perhaps, much of the old canonical exclusiveness of print. Some poet that I read years ago said that, in order to develop, a poet needed at least one friend whom he had to convince of his poetry. Early on, in an epigram, Pound said, 'I write these poems for four people…'

PMcC: What would you say really got you going with poetry? Was it partly the Bible, that great work of literature, that inspired you without you realising it, since it was more or less the only book you had at home, with both parents staunchly in the Salvation Army?

PD: The genius of poetry must work out its own salvation in an individual writer, Keats suggested. The reading aloud of the Bible, the King James, instilled a great feeling for the rhythms of English, an invaluable input for a writer.

My mother was not staunch in that respect of religion. She had a sharp tongue and wit in quoting the King James's version at my rather dithery father. Although she died when I was very young I still remember some of these sallies at the Sally Ann and other targets.

PMcC: I don't mean to concentrate too much on your life as I know that you feel (along with many present-day critics) that the life of a poet is ultimately irrelevant to his/her work, and that each poem must be 'free-standing'. But I have only recently realised that your mother died when you were twelve, and your father when you were still a student. Do you think it might have been an unconscious sense of bereavement, probably not fully realised, that pressurised you into writing poetry as a means of coping, of survival, and of creating the positive from ashes, as it were?

PD: I think the creative bug bit me before these events occurred, though it's a bit of a mystery to most poets how they catch it. The roads on the way to the canal and the fields where we played were named after the great British poets. That fascinated me in a deep unconscious way, I think. At primary school I had to read a poem by Thoreau about a squirrel and a mountain arguing. I expected that the mountain obviously would win. But it seemed the squirrel did. That perhaps was where the idea of dialogue and duologue began. Weirdly, at about the age of ten or eleven, I came across a Canterbury Tale in the Middle English. I soldiered through it, understanding little. It was like watching a dream where mysterious things happened and rather like being brought downstairs, more or less asleep, during air-raids and vaguely connecting with adult talk and feeling. But it fascinated me with words. My father used to say of certain Bible texts that they were beautiful. That set me puzzling over whether he meant the thought or the words as words were beautiful. It made me more aware of words as entities to be considered in themselves.

After she died we found a note-book of my mother's with balladic verses about my younger brother's development. Later, I discovered my elder half-brother wrote light verse for occasions in his family. So the maternal genes must have provided some impetus to poetry. Yet there may be some truth in your suggestion to account for an elegiac streak surfacing here and there.

PMcC: What do you think of the raw, personal 'I' in poetry? Some say this has now come back into fashion, albeit not in a full-blown confessional way, though it has been frowned upon for quite a while.

PD: I've used my own 'I' in very few poems, usually ones dedicated to or memorializing other poets, friends or family. But this 'I', *ego scriptor*, never went away from verse, from at least the Greeks onward. The phase of confessional verse was, in a back-to-front way, a species of aberrational showing off with it.

PMcC: Hasn't it been largely overlooked that if the poet's own personal voice is deeply lived, then the poem transcends the personal and becomes universal i.e. anyone's experience?

PD: I don't know whether it's been overlooked but the literature that moves me and most of us, I think, is a presentation of felt vicarious experience. Yeats once said that poetry was truth seen with passion. That, of course, includes passion seen with truth.

PMcC: In your book-length interview with Cynthia Haven (*Between the Lines*, 2005) you point out that all human beings, from no matter what culture, what era, what faith, share the great themes that you deal with – of 'heart-cry, birth, copulation and death, *lachrimae rerum*, and so forth'. You say these big themes are unpopular with modern audiences, and also with academics who require poetry 'they need to explicate'. What is your take on this now?

PD: No real change in that attitude – but I was speaking of paying audiences at readings. The silent audience of individual readers is another thing. Also I meant to indicate that it was accessible poetry that academics seemed to overlook, not the great themes. At least, I seem to remember a remark of John Bayley's in *Agenda*, saying he thought that's why my stuff was overlooked. It was too accessible to interest academics.

PMcC: What is your view of the plethora of Creative Writing departments in universities, where poems have to be written to order, as daily exercises? John Burnside, interviewed in the last issue of *Agenda*, states that he can work on a novel daily to a regular timetable, but that poems have to be waited for.

PD: He's right. That's why poetry can't be a career. Verse might be, especially in these festive, creative days. Poetry is a vocation. You have to have an inner drive for poems; it can be helped along sometimes but not injected by outside input. Many creative writing and festival activities have turned literature into more of a social event than an individual thing.

PMcC: I like the way you have said that the reader should always just eavesdrop on a poem, while remaining invisible. Aren't you here pairing up the reader with the writer who has to have a kind of lightness, and to listen to the inner ear when writing the urgent poem? The reader who then creatively has to make the read poem his/her own?

PD: The poet is the first reader of the poem that he has 'eavesdropped' into it. He then discovers in reading it if it is 'truable' in the mind of other readers. In the bicycle-wheel sense: does it run true, does it need truing? Collingwood suggested that the intelligence has its own emotions. Alvarez used to say or cite that an intellectual was a person to whom ideas were emotionally necessary.

PMcC: Exactly. The feeling intellect and the thinking heart. What do you think poetry's main role is in our society today?

PD: It is vastly diminished as a social influence. To pinch a religious Fundamentalist concept: a person has to be 'converted' to and by a poem, as was always the case. When that happens it's one of the ways we escape the internal exile in our own heads. Mass conversions, if they happen, are frequently teenage or fashionable flashes in the pan. But the contemporary world, with its information technology, celebrity culture and 'mediacracy', seems to have no pressing social or personal *need* for conversion. Creative writing groups can turn verse-writing into a species of the prevalent 'mehaviour' of the period while creating a sort of generic verse-product. 'Oh, I wouldn't bother writing a poem if I couldn't finish it in an afternoon,' one would-be poet said to me.

So poems survive as an unprotected species. They whisper in a few gadget-plugged ears and others: 'That passed; this will.'

PMcC: Intimacy seems essential to your work. WS Milne praises you for articulating 'the intimacies we find unspeakable'. This surely is one of poetry's biggest challenges: to express the unspeakable.

PD: It depends what is meant by unspeakable. A real poem is like a rare word for which there are no synonyms or homophones. I think WS Milne was citing or recapping a remark of DM Thomas. But I don't know how to answer this question. Poetry as an entity does not exist. Poems do. Some of the confessional poets seemed to search for unspeakable things to say. All a poet can do is to write the poem that whispers in his ear as powerfully and exactly as he can. I think it was Pound who wrote a clear image of what you seem to mean, saying that the poet's task was to make a statement such as 'Get me the sort of Rembrandt I like,' as clear as 'Buy me a pound of Braeburns.' I've adapted his terms. Perhaps to skew lines of my own a bit poetry at best can be: 'The blazon everywhere of unaccountable fire,/ unretellable by the symmetricating mind.'

PMcC: You are a great traditional and innovative formalist, both in your own poetry and in your translations. You say in an essay on Stanley Burnshaw (*Agenda*, Vol 21 No4/Vol 22 No1, Stanley Burnshaw Special Issue): 'The danger of a writer of theory is that he may allow his theories to swamp his creative work'. Have you ever felt a danger in your own work of form overtaking the content, as if the corset might shrink the body inside? Of the control of the logos overtaking instinct? Of the dichotomy between the bard and the poet?

PD: No. As Auden suggested the danger with form is rather in its facility not its constriction. It can be too easy and, in later life, new, untried and invented forms can provide renewed creative fire. Coleridge said of Donne that the wheels take fire from their motion. That means that the axles haven't been greased or lubricated. Look what happened to the villanelle form in *Local Habitation*. (I have hated repetitive forms all my life and that's what happens, splintered villanelles.) Someone asked Yeats where he got his extraordinary ideas from and he said it was in looking for the next rhyme. Valéry said, in later life, a rhyme-coincidence could start a poem. Form is like a bicycle. If you can't balance it you fall off. If you can, you can soon ride for miles. You don't have to say: how the hell do I do this, every time you go for a spin. Hardy, formally odd enough, spoke of there being a 'sincerity of form'. Form has its own creative fire for many poets. As I suggested to Cynthia Haven, poems seem to choose their own form.

PMcC: How important is rhythm to you?

PD: It's the rhythm that carries the conviction of a poem.

PMcC: Your work is full of wordplay, twisted clichés, puns, homonyms, of linguistic gymnastics and metaphors that speak meanings. Also your own vocabulary is particular to you and recognisable in any poem of yours.

PD: Well, I wouldn't think I'm the only user of such devices of language, and good and bad poets are usually recognisable in their vocabulary, ways of approach, and shaping. Coleridge wrote, of a line of Wordsworth, that, if he found it as a scrap in the desert, he would instantly exclaim, 'Wordsworth'. But as for word-play, one has only to listen to contemporary dialogue, banter and repartee, confrontation on trains, buses, the terraces to see how much of that goes on in ordinary life not just books.

PMcC: Let us turn to your translations. In the same essay on Burnshaw, you say that a translator is judged in two ways: 'first, by his choice of poem; secondly, by the skill of his version'. Can you account for your choice of poets to translate: Dante, Villon, Corbière, Laforgue, Valéry, translations from the Tamil? Will you ever tackle a living foreign poet who writes in free verse?

PD: The general pedigree of the French tradition of poetry, as usually considered, is called into doubt by the down-to-earth, mongrel energy of the poets I chose to do. The formal problem is like hanging in the morning. It clarifies the mind the night before it. The Tamil attracted my interests in dialogue. Albert Schweitzer said the best biographies of Jesus in his period were written out of hatred. Perhaps that's what drew me to Dante – and then there's the poetry, the brilliance of the terza rima. My wife said it was the biggest cross-word puzzle that I could find to keep my mind engaged while teaching. Truer than she meant perhaps, no punster.

No more translations. I may tinker with odd one-off drafts still lying about. I don't translate much free verse because it doesn't seem to challenge my mind-set. I wrote of the difficulties of translating more or less contemporary and free verse in the introductory essay 'Translating – or Mugging' for Brian Cole's translation of Bartolo Cattafi, *Anthracite,* Arc, 2000.

PMcC: I think you have said that translations are useful for a poet in that they can be worked on in lean times when the muse seems far away and the poems that demand to be written do not appear. How useful for your own poetic output have you found translating?

PD: It's not something one can answer now; who can tell what or how I would have written if I'd never translated? At most it broadened the mind, I suppose, as travel broadens the bum.

PMcC: Does trying to get inside a foreign poet's skin link to what you say is the imagined 'I' in many of your poems? This negative capability?

PD: I don't know. You have to have a rapport of some sort with your source poets. All I can say is that, when you start on someone like Villon, for example, it becomes as obsessive as your own poems to get the thing right. I put a ballade about the mystery of it all at the front of the current translation.

P McC: Going back to Burnshaw, who was a great theorist and poet – you, too, are an incisive intellectual as well as a poet. You have written many challenging, sometimes even self-avowed acerbic essays and reviews.

Since you specialise mainly in the lyric, did you experience, when writing verse-dramas, a certain freeing whereby the intellect could more directly and obviously be employed both in the lines of the characters and in the symbols and images used theatrically?

PD: Well, not really. As we've said, dialogue and duologue always attracted my imagination; verse-drama was another technical challenge to engage the imagination with it. *Cell* kicked off from Shakespeare's Richard II's soliloquy when he was in jail. Among other things it became also a chance to see whether stress metre could better reflect modern speech than blank verse could. *Sephe* did similar things. It began from four sonnets and then incorporated sonnet form as in early Shakespeare, and other buried forms in its dramatic development. It also allowed me to see how song could arise more dramatically. *The Dark Voyage* was a sort of cryptic response to Elgar's 'Dream of Gerontius'. It began as an opera text for a composer friend. It used pararhymed, Anglo-Saxon alliterative metrics. I was rather pleased to hear that Michael Alexander, translator of Anglo-Saxon, thought it worked rather well. There's also a modern play, *The Demiser*, in the same metre, that I haven't published yet. I don't suppose it will see the light of day now. It's a new departure: a pale black comedy.

PMcC: In that first verse-drama, *Cell*, the cell is allegorical for the cell of a totalitarian state and also of the cell of the self, or of your own mind. In depicting Everyman or modern man in this work with horrifying humour, were you wanting to highlight your conviction about the solipsism of human experience? And also of the modern alienation of man from moral and political systems?

PD: I think the play does many things, but it's not for the author to specify limits on the readers' interpretation of drama. Valéry said his poems meant whatever the reader thought or discovered they meant. Drama isn't a signpost; it's more like a score in music.

PMcC: In *Sephe*, the second verse-drama, based on the myth of Persephone, the haunting line 'your songs suspending hell' would seem to apply to you as a poet, accompanied by the determination of your survival (anyone's?) as a voice: 'I vow my voice in this/To foxglove, beech and pine/ Their form be tones of mine/To brighten every distance'.

PD: Not quite in those terms. You are downgrading the Eurydice / Orpheus input, Dicia and Fewsey. It may seem a bit of a cheek trying to write lyrics for Orpheus but I got myself into that bind. The lines you quote are a variant of the myth that the animals listened to him. (The plays have all been revised recently and may get collected with luck.)

PMcC: You have told me recently that you have made more money from writing carols than from any of your poetry. Ironic that you are writing carols, when you claim to be a confirmed atheist.

PD: Yes. I'm always surprised that Christians don't do it better. But atheist church composers do pretty well too. (Look back to what Schweitzer said above.) Some writer said that the most Christian passage in English literature was composed by the atheist Marlowe for the death of Faustus: 'See, see where Christ's blood streams in the firmament,' and so on. For my part, that early Christian indoctrination has served well, I suppose. Most of the classical myths have now lost their oomph. 'The myth kitty's empty,' said Larkin. This myth seems to have fizzled into a bit of life. Besides that, I have composer friends who seem to need and like my texts. So recently I seem to have slipped into co-authoring of sorts.

PMcC: Since moving to Wales a few years ago, you have developed an interest in dowsing and, indeed, are just completing a book in prose on it. Do you envisage this dowsing and also Wales – the land of Song, after all! – as springboards to further poems?

PD: There aren't any springboards for my poems. They sneak up on one. If a poem landed on the board it would dive or fall off and I can't swim. And, while on the topic of water, dowsing was an interest before arrival in Wales. That book started in a strange way. A life-long friend, a physicist, had been researching into the actual science that might make water-finding, the location of minerals and archaeological remains, work, investigating low frequencies that seem to be involved. We wanted to know *how* it might work. We weren't trying to explain the weird, esoteric end of dowsing, which we termed 'divining'. Although previously I used to tease him about his dowsing, I agreed to ghost the book for him. But he showed me I could actually dowse so I began repeating some of his experiments, thinking I should know something of what I had to write about. After a few chapters were drafted, he decided we should be co-authors. That's as far as we have reached at the moment. I don't think dowsing will turn up in poems but who can say?

PMcC: Will you go on writing poetry, drug that it is, for both sustenance and communication, until you drop? And be content to be known down the centuries as one of England's finest lyric poets?

PD: I have to write any poem that turns up. As for reputation after death, I shan't be here to know. Besides, with what humanity is doing now, there may not be any more centuries. 'The whole universe is the sport of my mad mother Kali.' As Beckett wrote in a character: 'I can't go on; I'll go on.' There isn't an option. Or much time.

PMcC: In a poem for David Jones, 'Old Poet on a Rainy Day', from your early powerful collection, *Mortal Fire*, you refer to the 'lonely art' of poetry. I am sure we will be able to say of you, along with England's major poets, 'and peace becomes their books, themselves'.

PD: Ah, it will be the famous RIP and not of the van Winkle type. Thanks for your patience.

Peter Dale

Memorial

Not this see-through stuff of memory. Rock,
that's what I need, granite. No more black lace
like winter saplings linked across the sky.
– This saffron blurring. – Something I can knock
the roughness off for years and yet still trace
your fine features; something I cannot ply
with drinks, a slim throat I cannot choke.
Your mountain-force of hair in the sun-smoke.

Above the eye-lash, single ply of cord.
Dove shadow in its curve; the arching brow –
who else saw that? strongbacked as a fish leaps.
How clear it is, and clean out of the mind's hoard.
How real ... love, is it you? Is it you now?
Let it be stone, love, where the flesh creeps.

Reprinted from *One Another*, in *Edge to Edge, Selected Poems*, 1996, by permission of Anvil Press Poetry Ltd.

Trio

Dan   Gill   Jo

      You thought you'd know her – by your dying day.
      How green her eyes, so dark her voice and low.
      You won't admit the memories that stay.

Do those years count? You'd thought there was a way.
You had such friends and plans. Your watch was slow.
You thought you'd know her till your dying day.

           The windows you looked out of – kids at play.
           The blossom on the cherry. Was it snow? indicate
           You cannot hug the memories that stay.

Who keeps a record of what is to pay.
The zeroes mount, and no line's drawn below.
And to your credit just a dying day.

      No glass can mirror absence turning grey.
      And what you see is nothing much to show.
      You do not choose the memories that stay.

Whatever you betrayed time will betray.
      The fonts outlast the names that we bestow.
You thought you'd know her till your dying day.
You do not want the memories to stay.

Note: The indentation of the lines indicates the speaker/thinker of the lines: the man, Dan, is unindented, the first indent is Gill, the second Jo. They are not necessarily in each other's presence.

Reprinted from *Local Habitation*, 2009, by permission of Anvil Press Poetry Ltd.

Song: The Valley

In the valley of the lilies long ago
      you walked with me those days that outlast years.
The rain-weighed branches sprinkled all below
      with glistening drops that were not tears.

While the season of the lilies comes and goes
      I walk along those days that haunt the year,
lilies that have to pass as your frail ghost
      beside the willows' long green weir.

Yet the willows do not weep; the river's course
      erodes the valley with its flood and flow.
The lilies have no passion, no remorse.
      What could a shade from Lethe know?

Voice Over

Well, I have come back.
There's nothing much to say.
Settled? Let's not speak.
It wasn't an odyssey.

You couldn't divine my way.
I've no clue to your life.
We split; no how or why,
no purchase on old love.

But we've bent the years back.
This is where we began.
Let's sit it out. Don't speak.
How it's all overgrown.

You tried to gather in,
I seem to remember once,
a leaf of every green,
oak, ash, sorrel, quince.

Hundreds of English grasses.
Tints enough for you,
the sedges, reeds and rushes?...
My leaves all folio.

The spinney shadows, taller,
close faster than before;
the leaves are losing colour
to take another fire.

Soon we must go away.
How broken is our old oath,
sworn with all reason why,
to put the earth between us.

Reprinted from *Da Capo*, in *Edge to Edge, Selected Poems*, 1996, by permission of Anvil Press Poetry Ltd.

Mary Fitzpatrick

Our Fortune's Made Up of our Friends

But we, for one moment out of what measureless abundance of time, burnt there triumphant. The moment was all; the moment was enough. And then I, as a wave breaks, surrendered.

Virginia Woolf: The Waves

We come to the altar of chrysanthemums and waves
Where each yellow explosion is followed by a mild concussion.

Candles and incense utter 'Transform'
Yet much remains. Here at the altar of persistent time

Memory shuffles and whirrs. Our histories merge –
Each vivid thirst becomes our shared

Understanding. We bend to the altar
To offer our gifts – the last conversation,

Garden fragrance, bony cheek brushed
By lips. All is desire wedded with time

Whose supplicants we are
   Oh stay each shining day

Attempting to slow the flickering minutes
   'We went out like sparks in burnt paper'

While to their great melting we pray.
   Remember me, remember me.

Note: *'We went out like sparks in burnt paper'* – this phrase in the penultimate stanza is also from *The Waves*.

The Empty Bed

Immaculate, sheathed in old sheets
so welcoming, virginal
without you. What matter now
the floral weave, or lavender-
scented sachet. Ground stone
of your mattress a presence. Harsh ticking –
buttons or spite. Under the bed
you stored up goods, blessings, seeds.
She watered the lawn so you
could lie in it. You cut the weeds
so she could sleep.

Frank hinge. Legs askew. You
were her headache, her fireplace.

Sheets

Adrift on your white sea
The swells of sails, pillowed by a huge
Wave of feathers, adrift
In your black day of foam
Ocean oh ocean
Where are you? Briny green soup
Ocean, oh ocean – how far away?
Laving your pale skin
In inky green, sailing,
Bobbing on the feathered swells,
Adrift in your white sea.

May Altar

The tiny pillars of my girlhood May altar
Were paper rolls covered in foil,
creased silver reflecting
the roses: yellow and pink, ivory
furnishings, a whole room awash
in curtained light, and the small statue
of Virgin Mary.

                Mother,
what Ionic or Doric columns
can I build you now? When bells toll
over the fields at dusk, *Ave, Ave*
you turn your palms up to the clouds.

Patient grace – now I understand
why we worship
your rare gift
        as does the sufferer on her final bed
        turn up her palms when medicines fail
and how in the darkened room
your light can be there
as roses, simply roses, suffuse the air.

The Mole

The mole fumbles quietly
Knocking into roots and rocks
Clearing each encounter she crosses
One clawed scoop at a time.

You drive to doctor appointments
Uncover the world of oncology
One visit, one pamphlet ...

The mole misses what I see of the oak
Misses spring's gay profusion.
She leaves her telltale hump;
Her blindness tempers us to mercy.

Underworld's warden watches our return
Rings a rosy of the ashen fallen
As we choose a casket, plot, or urn.
Mole's alive in dirt.

We stumble in the upper world
A fog blanketing our heads
We learn the path of our return –
Tunneling in.

Coda

Little mower, turnstile keeper, rock turner –
black genius of the blind alley
        silken sweatshirt, worm sucker, earth
      mover, shovel paw. Nose a lantern
           held before you in the dark.
              Rootthrower, hill builder, rock licker –
            moving tonight,
            no forwarding address.

Robin Houghton

River Ouse, Rodmell, 1941

The first she prises out, clenched in bindweed:
reluctance adds to its appeal.

And there: not so large as to burst pockets,
several flints conspire

their surfaces glass-perfect, all the better
to slip in without fuss.

From mud, she frees a stump of the fat chalk Down
walked each day, as worn

as the worsted that parcels up her reedy body
ready for anchoring.

Pebbles lean into her, take us they say, take us,
the floods are coming

but like Noah she must leave some behind,
the unbelievers.

John Griffin

Wonderland

A ship ran aground and foundered
in a bottle, its mast was split,
the hull was holed, the prow
ploughed into glass and sank,
until the genie of memory
uncorked its sunken timbers:

When you lay dying, grandfather,
your rare collection
of opal and turquoise bottles
were arrayed like an armada
across your dresser top –
A charter from the *HMS Victoria*
hung in a frame above your head,
and beside it a portulan chart
of Raleigh's Azores.
Your pennants hung at half-mast,
and all your accoutrements
were at rest – your pipe
poised in its stand,
your pince-nez and compass,
your shaving kit and cut-throat,
your Bible and Oxford miniature
of Marvell and your pocket watch
that filled the room with its antique tock.
I saw your feet in the port-hole mirror
as well as my own face, distorted,
jaundiced and waxen-hued.

A face shimmered starry-eyed
out of a mirage of tears
and rose from an oasis of goodbyes:
You came into unattainable focus,
a golden-haired boy
with tears in your eye –
In the room a headless,

footless mounted horse
stood on guard:
A Singer Sewing Machine
cast it shadow on the wall,
and the penumbra
of the funeral candle climbed
on top like an armoured knight –
the needle made a unicorn
of the phantasmagoria,
and presently the boy was at Elsinore
seeing off a dead king.

The Waves

i.m. Virginia Woolf

The mercurial deep is pregnant with plankton
and sunlight can't seep through. Krill abound.
Now come leviathans sifting and combing
the currents with their teeth, and now their killers,
undulating, unstoppable, determined as death.

> *Her silk hems whisper across the flagstone floor.*
> *Embroidered hassocks sit on a hutch by the window.*
> *Her sarcophagus reeks of lime and Bakelite.*
> *Delphiniums gird it. She wonders is there a way*
> *to mine death's walls with silent prayer.*

Everything swims through the death of the whale.
He bleeds on all sides and the sick world enters
the ribbed cathedral of his savaged, mangled maw.
His torpid trunk sinks beneath the roil and shock
of the waves and lies felled on the ocean floor.

> *Her dream is still on though her conscious mind*
> *is beginning to register the ambient dins of day:*
> *pneumatic iambs syncopated by traffic's trochees*
> *and the spondees of an urgent siren punctuated*
> *by the dactyls of her plaintive, measured cries.*

But soon the turquoise sea will be whole again
and sunlight will net the shimmering shallows.
The killers will return to surf the sands for seals
and then will hurl themselves back out to sea –
one mistimed plunge and they'll maroon to drown in air.

> *What's inside her dark is a bulb that hasn't been lit yet,*
> *like a bud asleep within its chrysalis of bloom,*
> *but when she wakes vertiginous she sees the birds are dying*
> *on the terraces, shocks of stage fright ripple through her*
> *and she falls like a white leaf disappearing into her own dark.*

Inland across the heaths the wind is peopled with the skeletons
of whales, rogue clouds full of a green decrepitude
darken into floods and now pillars of truncated rainbows
(sunk in osier beds where the bohemians come to die),
rise up and strangle the roots of the sea-bred winds.

> *Feathers float through her Platonic green but still perceive*
> *themselves in flight: what is it animates this remembrance*
> *built into bones? By quirks and fits her love shapes the urns*
> *that turn on the wheels of longing, tears wet and taper the clay*
> *and lighted candles float by on the water's surface.*

The coastline fades. The light of evening plunders
the ocean's arabesques and the bald dunes clutch
their few remaining strands of wild grass. Arrowroot and ficus,
sage and juniper all feed off the whale's beached bones,
a haze rises off the hills and bees forage among the grapes.

> *She is trapped by her fears and knows there is no courage*
> *in posing: one kiss and she might've been an undine or mermaid,*
> *but she is dying instead with the summer on a bed of roses.*
> *The street lights cast their lurid shadows into the trees,*
> *and the possums browse and drub the graveyard grass for grubs.*

Marek Urbanowicz

Mr. Audley's Daughter

Sometimes she could almost hear him,
spectral in her ear, or even
feel his presence like a mist, damp
on her skin but not visible.

There were times when she was so sure
that he was there, could taste his voice
like the peat glow of malt whisky
smoking on her tongue, its embers

dropping, fizzing from time to time,
firing her iced heart till it lit
from within with its own pale light
to thaw in strangely charmed places,

portals in ordinary times:
her mother's house (his French widow)
or 'holes in the wall' where she drew
not paper notes but messages,

revenant, timeless, slipped between
the strange and charmed quarks, new-minted
from that other place where he drew
cartoons of cricketing angels,

races in Elysian time
between three-legged sacked devils
or fights, fists brimming with brimstone
just for the sheer damned hell of it.

Perhaps Time itself was liquid,
soft as Dali's watch as she watched,
like an émigré, English life
from behind her half-exiled eye,

saw that this time, that table, chair
dissolve as if on LSD,
slip past the portals of birth, death
 in an indivisible mist,

an amorphous glow of No Time,
where quarks have no bottom or top,
where her father was still present,
where the heart is luciferous.

I watch her in her time, juggling
children, houses, grieving, suitors,
am unable to pass this glass
to give my invisible gift.

Instead, I hand her these strange, charmed lines,
Platonic, revenant like kites
to hoist us up past glass, mists, quarks
to be other, undead, timeless.

Gill McEvoy

Laying the White Rose

just one, lengthwise on his grave,
its head where she supposed his head
would be, was what she'd meant to do.

Her fingers of their own free-will
undid the rose, shedding petals
on the ground in which he lay.

She counted as they fell: one for each
sorrow, cruelty.
Still there were petals screwed

around the rose
so she counted unfamiliar abstracts:
happiness, loyalty, trust –

came then to *forgiveness*,
laid the little that remained
of that white rose along the grave.

Its yellow stamens at his head
glowed like a puny torch of gold
as if there were still some hope for *love*.

Conservatory

In the glass white leaves are etched,
fixed like water frozen in its flow.

Outside, the autumn trees, the rain.

Float out. Rest in the branches of
oak and sycamore,

stretch out your limbs,
receive the light rain on your skin.

Fallen leaves have settled on the grass.

Soon worms will pull them down,
etch them into earth.

This is your time. Now,
among trees and rain.

Trust. You will be held.

Kevin Cahill

Peaseblossom

for Pamela Thorby

Drifting in like pollen, she has already begun to play
before the play begins. In her Tudor haircut, in her Puck gown,
she sways like a sunflower. Tittuping through movements
like a honeybee, and moving on, she is a hare's-foot key-ring,
a handsel pouring with music given from one bough to another,
her charism clouded in cannons and collapsed buildings.

For this is an Englishwoman, playing Campion, playing baroque
and early music seated in the start of the trouble:
the ruffs who found the marches and keys
of the old soundbox, the musette and drums of their coming,
the rowan rods in the shape of men snapped and peeled
and the unfit mouths at the holes.

Now the mouth has come, like a new moon,
a rod picked from the Pleiades, a mouthpiece
picked by Corin; carrying all of us in the old religion again:
the corn pipes of Ceres, the notation awoken
from its long hallucination, brought back to honey-sprees,
back to the piping lung full of woodbines and wassails.

For what came with guns comes with recorders now:
the greaves come like Robin Goodfellows, cobwebs
come like stems: the syrinx squeezed like a snowdrop's lobe –
its blown nib feeding us on mulberries and green figs,
September balsams, the bulbs hidden blossom now in her belling:
its rhubarb: its foreign stick of sweet Castello, Bassano, Dowland.

Reconciliation

You're meant to wait until they're dead
before you forgive your fathers.
When mine died and they carried him off
in the car it was a surprise to see him again
at the door wiping the scar on the top of his head.

The gods gave him back to me
to forgive him for something
and so he survived in the keepnet by the weedy pool
where I thought of what to forgive him for
and then to throw him back in.

Surrounded by police-tape or chalked on the floor
we sit down for something to eat
together like incidents at a crime-scene
and everyone is afraid to touch one another and no one gets
to touch his mouth.

What did he ever do that he had to come back?
Because he had us? Because he made us
as well as a cabinet – with the care
that would go into that, and no more.
Because he loved with that love and no more?

With what he could: the love
a tradesman would use to make a stool, measuring it,
finding a tool, to fashion it, a tongue of it there
only waiting for the groove to house itself in.
And so we stand for the photograph like strangers

as he comes back in a swaddle
with his head bandaged up after the haemmorrhage
and keeps himself in the keepnet for us like a toy-bear
on perpetual display. Something to discomfort a child with,
to pull out in the dark and say

this is not enough. This is enough.
The clay pipe, the Sunday stew, the D.I.Y.,
the old bones, the match programme, the bones,
the bingo nights, the jazz of Saturday nights making food:
a music as weak and insufficient as a wafer for our mouths.

Chris Fletcher

125 mph

I trace routes through artex on the ceiling
flying upside down (in bed) over alps.

Lights out, you're profiled in the doorway.
Lying there I watch you take rope,

tilt back your head, open wide, and
feed the impossible length down.

A simple trick of shadow and light, my
need to believe neatly tied up. But you

had real tricks too: sending a shoe up a
kite string, divining water –

the splayed stick gripped
tight as it squirmed around –

or counting to the top speed of your Rover,
lane-lines fired at me like tracer.

Keys

I threw away the keys
lined up in the pouch
like little silver fishes,
and hooked up my own.

They would have opened
suitcase, padlock, desk,
the garage with your old
bike and over-oiled tools,

or the place you kept
the Webley we'd use
to pop the ghosted
bulbs you'd stash away,

then shoot straight up,
listening, hands on head,
for that unheard
drop of lead.

I kept the gun and some
film found in your camera,
tightly wound with
memory, I imagine.

Warren Stutely

ars nova

birds are sung
illuminations

struck ornaments
in cool wings of ink

the craft of forms
abstract

& neumes
crystal as mill streams

galleries of morning surface cubist
trifles

manuscript
an air of quills jig and glitter cord grey

brilliance
salting a quick voice of sung light

a single gleam of knife
sculpting

antiphons
sound as a volumed page

querning a wash of stone
word freshed

metric strictures
thick in vowelled organum language

on the tongue of chant
bright mineral rim struck morning

vocal white notations
scholar norms of a new art

song coast

bright form january
mark

glance
birds as sung illuminations

a great song shrill
crisp

sequence as an angel morning
thirsts

a fleece of urgency
shingle

struck sea ornaments
consonant

on the tongue of chant
white bell

and mansion a link of
psalms

spokes a cloud bright voice of
coast

horizon
verse and syllable a light of quill

lisp such galleries and manuscript
of sound

gasp opal
water figures sentence rain

brilliance
a salt knife stroke

platonic gospels a soft blue shoal
kestrel a gust of morning

grey trace fish and nets of absolutes
spring   flower   and blow

Eleanor Hooker

54

Rain clouds unfurl, fumble on the Clare shore, low set
to the water. Checking the line our crew calls 'Squall',
counting down as breathy patches darken on the surface,

warning signs as we harden up to weather. And then it's
upon us. 54 heels and we sit up, hang out, and take
all the lifts we can. On Port tack with no rights, 45

charges up on Starboard. Whispers, 'We'll dip below her'.
I ease the sheet as you bear away, and with a hair breadth
our timbers almost kiss, six feet visible only beneath their

boom. Before the mark slips back in time we tack onto
starboard. A giant gust retches across our bow and the
shrouds wail. A low moaning, a keening for the wind

vibrates through the forward thwart, along the gunwale,
varies its pitch with every flurry. Our tell-tales, wool from
Granny's sweater, say we're pinching, so we ease the pain.

Round the mark onto a run, a lolling death roll, so we slight
a drop of plate and sheet in. Balanced now, 54 surges into
a steady sprint and crosses the finish, panting, upright and intact.

Note: 54 is a Shannon One Design (SOD), an 18ft clinker built wooden vessel, with one mainsail of 144 square foot and a modified Gaff Rig. She is sailed three up. SODs are sailed only on Lough Derg and Lough Ree. The boat numbers begin at 32 because that was the favourite number of the captain of the first fleet of SODs. 54 was built in 1928 and before us, was sailed by Granny who won many races in her. 45 was built in 1926 and is sailed by our cousins, the Sanders.

Recovery

He's overdue, that's all we know.
As the lifeboat tugs the reins of snow
blown steeds, crew take each new wave
on a rising trot. The rhythmic pitch

of our engine's blades is the sound
of hope in tortured air. Overhead
the sky lies low with blame, seeking
solace in the speckled mirror of the lake.

We search the run and flow of current
winds, racing points on our compass.
Very soon we find his skiff, holed
and broken by the gales. And then,

close by, we find him too. Drowned.
Alone and still. We stop and bow our heads,
all silent now, even the wind has stilled its
ragged wail. But this is no Ophelian scene,

there are no fragrant flowers here, February
insists on monochromes of brown and ash,
with wintered reeds and lough his only cradle.
Gone is colour from this life. Gray lake

infused, a waxen absence dyes his face
and hands. His eyes. We break our gaze
as overboard into this other scene we slide,
to gather up, tender to the last of rites.

Treading water, the wind resumes its desolate
howl, we pass our hands along and lift him towards
a journey's ending, knowing well that passage home,
he'd crossed alone some days before.

Songs of the Sea

At Kilmore town, ancient carols are sung,
Legends say the sea will drown their town.
Casting stones into the sea is wrong,
Storm-crested waves drag silent sail down.

Legends say the sea will drown their town,
A silver coin beneath the mast brings luck.
Storm crested waves drag silent sail down,
church bells sound when sinking ships are struck,

A silver coin beneath the mast brings luck.
true to say, what the sea wants, it gets,
church bells sound when sinking ships are struck,
a curlew's flight makes faired sailors fret.

True to say, what the sea wants, it gets,
casting stones into the sea is wrong,
a curlew's flight makes faired sailors fret,
at Kilmore town, ancient carols are sung.

Robert Smith

Aphasia

Words like scattered type
pursed in the mouth's enactment,
their vowels uninked,

singling out labials,
working into their lineaments
frustration's bolus

for want of fluency,
a palaver racing in the brain,
scanning its own defects;

the duress adamant,
each gesture epic in its recourse,
flailing a dry nib on the air.

Telephone

Intolerable then,
the black ice after midnight,

the mental arithmetic of stars
as his finger trawls on the dial:

in the exposure of her voice
a dwarfed sympathy.

Stuart Medland

One Moment

One moment…

You were holding me up
In the frame of the window
As if only yourself and
This child were in focus

To watch the Marines,
All sailorly, on the
Parade ground and
Wait for the one on
His own by a flagpole
To play us the tune only
You knew the words for …

'… *the Mose, oh,*
The Mose, oh, the
Mose, oh, the Mose …'

To do with a cat
That turned up on the
Doorstep after a storm.

And the next …

I was flying along
The Kent coast road
Beneath the power
Station that I never
Dared look up at –

On the long-nosed bicycle seat
You'd spannered to the crossbar
Just enough to balance me
Between your pumping knees –
With nothing for my hands to
Do but fiddle with the bell
And rainy wind upon my face,
Your big breath pedalling
In my ears – from Ramsgate

All the way to Deal.

Fingerprints

You were a specialist
In Scenes of Crime
And Fingerprints.

We learned them too;
*Whorl and double-Loop
And bifurcated Arch –*

Sat with you, fascinated
By their shoelace-loopy
Rollings that would always
Nose up underneath the
One above and make it
Topple over, rather like
Your own wry eyebrows
That we liked to watch.

We traced along them,
Wanting them to be
A proper maze as if
This was a Puzzle
Book. There never was
A satisfactory solution
To those Fingerprints. We

Understood that you could
Easily identify a person
By a single fingerprint, that
You could tell a good man
From a bad one, though it
Wasn't by their kind of
Pattern – which I never
Fathomed. When you

Frowned, I didn't know
If it was that you didn't
Want us touching
Bad men's fingerprints
Because they might be
Touching us as well, or
Whether it was time for you
To concentrate. We were still

Learning to identify you properly.

Ford

Here is the pebble-shiny, sixpence-clinking water
Swilling thin across the road as if from buckets

At the ford – now turning muddy with the
Wet earth melting from the soft stream bank and
Slopping over Wellies onto socks. Gushing up
The rubber tyres and bodywork of cars come

Cleaving water noisily, while
You stand back a little, just a
Little. With a stick. *Still the Cornish
Magic of it stirs me; that a stream
Will swallow up a lane and maybe
Let it go again.* I've lost you in a sudden
Childhood of my own until I fasten to the

Slap and hollow-clonk of those black
Rubber Wellingtons at loose around the village,
Bored of fords and aimless as a Sunday,
Soggy socks around your toes, jumping
Halfway out of them to pull at dripping twigs
And let them spring their water everywhere.

I've found the Church. I turn to hear you
Running down and through the churchyard
After school, clanging the kissing-gate
(High on the hill as the tops of the trees) in
Front of brother Keith the moment he arrives and
Flying, helter-skelter, in between the gravestones,
Ducking yews, with arms akimbo to be somehow
On your feet still by the bottom of the damp and
Shady slope. *Stopping
At the sight of me* – One

Hand upon the cold and iron handle
Of the ship-thick woodworm door. Caught out –
Seeking a reminder of you that your Auntie Dot
Had asked should never be removed; a
Sticky-paper label with your name and age –

L Medland, 8 Years – written on it, stuck
Above just where, upon an ear-shaped hook
Behind a stack of chairs, you hung your
Choirboy surplice one last time
Some sixty years ago. I watch you
Backing off on dancing feet – composure
Quickly re-asserted – and now run to

Chase the schoolcap you've just thrown ahead to
Try to catch, with one look back at me before you
Swing the wrought-iron churchyard gates upon
Yourself and all those steps set wide and sideways-on
To mount a lady's horse from half-way down –
Another back at Keith, still catching-up, then

Quickstep down them, jumping three at once
To spot a landing on the lane and sprint,
Head down, up to Trequite. Your only thoughts

Of Auntie Dot (and brother Keith, of course) and tea.

Toughening Up

(your R.A.F. photograph)

It's you, all right, though

Not in the policeman's
Uniform we understood
You in and Mum ironed
All those dark-blue shirts

For. It is you
But so far back
You have not even
Learned to fly.

Or catch somebody
Else's eye. A
Thumping-
Hearted
Youngster,
Trying to set a
Soft face hard.

Choosing a manhood.
Closing your eyes and
Jumping in with both feet
So you'd have to learn to swim.

This was the way to toughen-up:
You let the Forces have you
(while you drove munitions lorries
through the last dregs of a war).

It wasn't as if you needed
Toughening-up again

And when the doctor
Dipped his finger
In the shadow of your eyelid

He took the time to tell us
That whatever you
Had dragged yourself
Through this time

Your heart was
Like an Ox's. It

Was all the rest.

Alfonso Reyes

Translated by Timothy Adès

Farewell

To Enrique González Martínez

Now once again advancing, the grim relentless woodman
despoils and lays in ruins the green and towering tree.
The best recourse is silence: the less we say the better,
locked in this confrontation with old iniquity.

Rather than raise the anguished laments of desolation,
it's better not to listen, it's better to forget.
The lamp still burns discreetly, by which he kept his vigil:
let no-one undeceive it, nor dare to quench it yet.

We know the wall grows weaker: already the eternal
looms through the veil transparent, we see it face to face;
let's join our hearts together, and make this last entreaty:
a truce, a pause; for friendship implores an hour of grace.

The poet roams about us so close we hear his footfall,
and still we may imagine, and dream that he once more
will come at any moment and re-appear among us,
and take his place at table, just as he did before.

We have no time for weeping, no time and no occasion,
won over by his bearing, his easy courtesy.
The poet's face of copper smiles down on us, all cheerful,
just like a moon emerging, enormous, from the sea!

© *Thanks are due to the Fondo de Cultura Económica*

Ballad of the Dead Friends

(At age 57)

Half-a-dollar, seven cents:
I am neither rich nor poor,
have no high ambition, nor
lowly lack of confidence.
Years, as such, I don't deplore,
they are neither sad nor scary,
but the way they steal my friends,
ply their broom behind the door,
sweep up Tony, Peter, Harry.

Pictures, keepsakes; these will be
all I have for company.
Days enjoyed, bright memory!
Old wine, gone: the wine today
doesn't give the same bouquet.
Peaceful readings, pleasant chat:
clear I needn't add to that.
Flow, my tears; it's right to cry:
Harry, Peter, Anthony.

Where is that enchanted night
going over Plato's *Phaedrus*,
when those teeming notes of Peter's
rained on us till it was light?
Tony's heaven-sent delight
or Mephisophelean guffaw;
Harry's prattle, like a river,
humour of the tranquil Zephyr;
integra dulcisque vita:
Harry, Anthony and Peter.

*Listening Muse whose lips are sealed,
sound the dirge, intone responses:
Peter, Tony, Harry, Alphonsus:
The fool survives, the wise are felled.*

† Enrique Díez-Canedo.
† Antonio Caso.
† Pedro Henríquez Ureña.

© Thanks are due to the Fondo de Cultura Económica

Avril Staple

If You Hadn't Died So Young

For Barry, 1997

If you hadn't died so young,
you might have become
lazy, strapped to a desk
with a telephone for a head,
kept trainers with unmarked tread
in the top left-hand drawer.

Your bass guitar collection
might have been relegated
to the loft along with records
and relevant posters
of obscure bands and artists.

You would probably have put on weight
preferring a 4x4 for the kids' run
and I doubt if you would ever consider
cycling from Bristol to Orpington,
the laptop being so cumbersome.

I wonder what you would have made
of the latest in telecommunications.
We could have skyped in the bath,
your friends and mine swapping
virtual farm stock on *facebook*.

After your first sprog
you might have looked me up –
found me greying in the same house
and asked in your Kentish drool
'How's it goin', toothy'.

Maureen Duffy

The Book of the Dead

We have come to peer at the dead, spiced up
eviscerated, parcelled out in Canopic jars
embalmed, bound, their rites of passage
painted on coffin wood, inside as well
as out before the last lid is hammered home
so they can follow correct etiquette
instructions on papyrus, plaster, shawl.

Their mouths are adzed open so the fluttering
Ba spirit can come and go. Did it hover
hawk or humming bird chirruping to come in?
And then the final lid, sculptural, pared
down to anonymity, sealed. So the Ba bird
must have passed, like neutrinos, singing
winging through matter. Last the boat, older
than Charon, crossing the dark waters
before the gates you must gain with your passport
spells, till, standing before the immortals
your heart hangs heavy from the scales weighing
good against bad. O love when they weigh
our hearts, whatever the judges, time
or tongues, let the scale tip that we loved.

James Aitchison

Chain of Being:
The Fellowship of Dead Poets

Towards the end of Book XI of *The Prelude*, having expressed his sadness and anger at France's betrayal of the ideals of the Revolution, Wordsworth abruptly changes his narrative focus and writes:

> But indignation works where hope is not,
> And thou, O Friend! will be refreshed. There is
> One great society alone on earth:
> The noble Living and the noble Dead.

Even allowing for the ambiguity of the fourth line above – are only some people noble, or is there nobility in all of us? – the lines affirm a community and continuity in life and death.

D.H. Lawrence confesses to a similar belief in community and continuity in a self-conscious passage in his Introduction to *Fantasia of the Unconscious* (1923):

> How many dead souls, like swallows, twitter and breed thoughts and instincts under the thatch of my hair and the eaves of my forehead I don't know. I am almost ashamed to say, that I believe the souls of the dead in some way re-enter and pervade the souls of the living.

One can understand that Lawrence, careful of his reputation as a visceral critic of life and literature, should feel embarrassed at admitting his belief in metempsychosis; the fact that he feels impelled to make the admission shows the strength of his belief in the transmigration of the souls of the dead into the living.

T.S. Eliot writes of communion with the dead and the unborn in his discussion of the family in 'The Class and the Elite' in *Notes towards the Definition of Culture* (1948). He refers to the immediate family, and he adds: 'But when I speak of the family, I have in mind a bond which embraces a longer period of time than this: a piety towards the dead, however obscure, and a solicitude for the unborn, however remote.' He states the need for a spirit of reverence for past and future life, and he explains: 'Such an interest in the past is different from the vanities and pretensions of genealogy; such a responsibility for the future is different from that of the builder of social programmes.' In effect, Eliot is asking us to revere the wider human family, humanity itself; and his phrase, 'the vanities and pretensions of genealogy', shows that his concern is unconditional, for human life and not for rank.

Human communion and continuity are recurring themes in the poetry and prose of Edwin Muir. In the lecture, 'Poetry and the Poet', in the posthumously published *The Estate of Poetry* (1962) Muir writes:

> The past is a living past, and past and present coexist: that also the imagination tells us. It opens the past to us as part of our own life, a vast extension of our present. It cannot admit that anything that ever happened among the dead is dead for us, or that all that men and women have done and suffered was merely meant to bring us where we are.

The past comes alive and becomes part of the life of the living when it is revivified by the imagination, which is not constrained by the usual division of time into past and present. Muir's other claim, or rather, his denial, in the quotation above – that all that people in the past have done is to create a chain of life that extends into the present – is prompted by his Christianity and his belief in the immortality of the soul. For some non-Christian readers it is enough to be aware of the continuity of the earthly succession of generations of people.

In British society there is a reluctance to speak openly about the dead. We allow a funeral oration for the individual, an annual Commemoration Day for those who died in war, and then there is silence. But the quotations above show poets speaking of the dead and the unborn as if they were members of the living community. Stephen Spender expresses the same kind of communion and continuity when he discusses the artist and the city in 'Inside the Cage' in *The Making of a Poem* (1955):

> A city should belong at the same time to the inhabitants, who use it, the dead who have invented forms which give pleasure to the eye, and the unborn in whom the delights enjoyed by the dead will live. In towns where the dead and the unborn are omitted, there are simply buildings and thoroughfares used by contemporaries.

That is not only a vision of the city but of the continuity and unity of successive generations of its inhabitants. C. Day Lewis in 'The Nature of the Image' in *The Poetic Image* (1947) extends the sense of community to every living thing as well as to the dead, and he states that the need for communion is an emotional need: 'man, even at his most individual, still seeks emotional reassurance from the sense of community, not community with his fellow beings alone, but with whatever is living in the universe, and with the dead.' The term, 'emotional reassurance', suggests a kind of dependence, whereas what Day Lewis describes is an interdependence of the living and the dead; his reference to the universe implies a concept of community that is cosmic in scale. Kathleen Raine too feels an affinity with dead poets; in the chapter, 'The Lion's Mouth' in *Autobiographies* (1973) she writes of the community of poets: 'Not living poets only, or principally, but the dead also are, in that sense, our own people in a way that for the critic is not so.'

These poets' experiences of communion with the anonymous dead seem wider and more conceptualized than the experience all of us feel about people we have known who are now dead. People whose lives are important to us, people alive and dead, are part of our identity in the most intimate way: they are represented in our minds as specifically encoded sets of neural networks. When a loved person dies, we feel the death as a lesion, a little death, in the designated set of networks. The networks that represent living people also represent them after their death; the fact of their death is encoded in the living network so that the dead continue to be represented, continue to live, in the mind of the survivor. Sometimes this inner representation is so vital that it is projected and seems to correspond momentarily with outer reality, as when a woman sees her dead husband alive and walking in the street. But this experience is clearly different from the sense of communion with the dead expressed by Wordsworth, Lawrence, Eliot, Muir, Spender, Day Lewis and Raine.

A sense of communion with the dead extends into the twenty-first century. Muriel Spark in an interview with Robert Hosmer published in *The London Magazine* (August/September 2005), was asked: 'How do you perceive your relationship to great writers of the past?' She replied: 'Well, I think if I was writing for anybody, I would be quite happy to write for the great past, for the great dead.' And in her Foreword to *All the Poems* (2004) Spark states: 'Although most of my life has been devoted to fiction, I have always thought of myself as a poet. […] My outlook on life and my perceptions of events are those of a poet.' Spark is one of the most recent in a long line of poets who have written about a sense of continuity and community with the dead.

Margaret Atwood expresses the same kind of affinity. In the title lecture in her Empson Lectures, *Negotiating with the Dead* (2002), she states that dead people persist in the minds of the living, and then she adds: 'All writers learn from the dead. As long as you continue to write, you continue to explore the work of writers who have preceded you; you also feel judged and held to account by them.' There is a particular continuity from dead to living writers, and the living writer is accountable to the dead. In 'Nine

Beginnings' in *Curious Pursuits* (2005) Atwood states that the writer is one of 'the community of writers, the community of storytellers that stretches back through time to the beginning of human society.'

Poets take account of the anonymous dead in something like the way in which a nation takes account of its Unknown Soldier, who represents the mass of dead soldiers. Poets know that we must not only take account of the dead but also listen to them; and when the dead speak to us we must respond. Indeed, Auden writes of communion with the dead as a sacrament without which we cannot be fully human. In 'Words and the Word' in *Secondary Worlds* (1968) he writes:

> Further, let us remember that, though the great artists of the past could not change the course of history, it is only through their work that we are able to break bread with the dead, and without communion with the dead a fully human life is impossible.

Listening and responding to the dead are such natural acts that a capacity for an inner dialogue with the dead must be part of the mind's design; and in that sense, hearing voices inside our head is not an aberration. We should feel that we are free to converse silently with the dead and even, in private places, to speak to them aloud. The cultural constraints against such dialogues have the effect of distorting the natural response into a shameful act; the constraints also have the effect of breaking one's sense of the natural continuity of generations.

*

Community and continuity of a different kind have been discovered by molecular biologist and other scientists working in the field of genetics. Genetic continuity originated with beginning of life on earth around three thousand million years ago; Homo sapiens, our most immediate ancestor, evolved around half a million years ago. The human time-scale could change as new discoveries are made, but the biological sequence from the beginning of life to the present is unbroken. Each of us inherits around three thousand million markers or letters of genetic material, DNA, in unique combinations. A loose comparison can then be made between the human genetic system and the human brain.

Every brain has the same structure, and to some extent the same infrastructure, but has unique combinations of around a hundred billion neurons and many millions of neural networks. Our personal genes decay, but each person in each succeeding generation will have a unique recombination of genes; our neurons and neural networks decay, but all our successors will have unique recombinations of neurons and networks. The diversity-in-unity of our earthly succession, genetic and neural, will continue into the indefinite future. These are facts of life. Could poetic communion and continuity also be factual?

Shelley overstates the case for poetic communion to such an extent that the modern reader might dismiss as hyperbole the reference in *A Defence of Poetry* to 'that great poem, which all poets, like the co-operating thoughts of one great mind, have built up since the beginning of the world.' A remarkably similar idea is expressed by Eliot, whose poetic views and values often differ from Shelley's. In 'Tradition and the Individual Talent' (1919), Eliot writes:

> No poet, no artist of any art, has his complete meaning alone. His significance, his appreciation is the appreciation of his relation to the dead poets and artists. You cannot value him alone; you must set him, for contrast and comparison, among the dead.

Virginia Woolf discusses a similar concept in 'A Letter to a Young Poet' in *The Death of the Moth* (1942). Woolf warns the young poet of the danger of adopting a false persona and of becoming 'a self-conscious, biting, and scratching little animal whose work is not of the slightest value or importance to anybody.' And then she adds: 'Think of yourself rather as something much humbler and less spectacular, but to my mind far more interesting – a poet in whom live all the poets of the past, from whom all poets in time to come will spring.' The concepts are attractive: all poems are part of a great universal poem, a living force that is continuously revitalized and extended by new poems. Equally attractive is the idea of a succession of poets whose unity of purpose is like one great talent or one great poetic self, continuously evolving but never losing sight of the original talent or self.

Robert Nye discusses just such a succession in his Introduction to *A Selection of the Poems of Laura Riding* (1996). He recalls his meetings with Riding in 1991:

> I shall never forget how at one point, after we had been talking of the ancient idea of the Great Chain of Being, she called me back urgently into her room to tell me that the Great Chain of Being consisted of poets. 'Poets inspire poets,' she said. 'From here in this room to Homer the Great Chain of Being stretches back.'

Nye's and Riding's words remind one of the doctrine of Apostolic Succession, the belief that there is a continuity of spiritual authority that begins with

Christ and his Apostles and has been transmitted continuously by popes and bishops ever since. Genetically, continuity is a fact of the human condition; poetically, the continuity is, like Apostolic Succession, a doctrine, a faith in a truth that is essentially imaginative or mystical but could also have a basis in fact. Establishing that basis, however, might prove impossible. No one reader could possibly trace the chain from its beginning to the present, because no one could read all the poetry that has survived from the time of Homer.

Riding, Nye and the other poets quoted above are referring to a spiritual or metaphysical community. I. A. Richards is hostile to the concept. In the final paragraph of the chapter, 'Four Kinds of Meaning' in *Practical Criticism* (1929), he repeats his complaint that too much of what passes for criticism of poetry is merely a projection of the critic's personal feelings. Richards states that 'eminent examples' of this kind of false reading are: 'Dr Bradley's remark that Poetry is a spirit, and Dr Mackail's that it is a continuous substance or energy whose progress is immortal.'

Andrew Cecil Bradley (1851-1935) was Professor of Poetry at Oxford University from 1901 to 1906, when he was succeeded by John William Mackail (1859-1945). Some of Bradley's views in his *Oxford Lectures on Poetry* (1909) – on meaning in poetry, the experience of a poem, the reader's presuppositions, and on poetry as discovery – are so similar to Richards's views in *The Principles of Literary Criticism* (1925) and *Practical Criticism* that one wonders why Richards complains about Bradley. Perhaps it is partly a matter of anthropology: a younger generation tries to establish itself by attacking the preceding generation. The words Richards objects to appear at the end of 'Poetry for Poetry's Sake' in *Oxford Lectures on Poetry*, where Bradley writes of poetry: 'It is a spirit. It comes we know not whence. It will not speak at our bidding, nor answer in our language. It is not our servant; it is our master.' If Bradley is wrong, then it follows that others who have made similar claims – Wordsworth, Shelley, Lawrence, Eliot, Muir, Day Lewis, Spender, Raine, Riding, and Nye – are also wrong. Clearly, the weight of opinion is against Richards. But what if it is merely received opinion?

Few poets today would claim that they are the latest links in the great chain of being that is the fellowship of dead poets. But most poets know that their work is not entirely secular and that the words 'spirit' and 'spiritual' can be applied to those functions of mind that include the sacred and creative impulses in interaction with the creative imagination. Poetry is a natural and inevitable expression of the human spirit, and a natural and inevitable outcome of mind and language. Poets will continue to respond to the same spiritual impulses; they will write in the same spirit, and poetry as an expression of that spirit will continue to renew itself into the future. We can argue, then, that poetry has a kind of immortality.

Auden in 'Making, Knowing and Judging' in *The Dyer's Hand* (1963) perfectly captures the triumph of poetry over mortality when he writes of 'a vision of a kind of literary All Souls Night in which the dead, the living and the unborn writers of every age and in every tongue were seen as engaged upon a common, noble and civilizing task.' Denise Levertov, like Auden, a British-born poet who settled in the United States, writes with a similar religious intensity in 'Some Duncan Letters – A Memoir and a Critical Tribute' in *New & Selected Essays* (1992), where she imagines a sacred fellowship of poets: 'If Poetry, the Art of Poetry, is a Mystery, and poets the servers of that Mystery, they are bound together in a fellowship under its laws, obedient to its power.'

The art of poetry is, indeed, a mystery, because language and mind are mysterious and because poetry is the celebration of and participation in mystery. When poets believe that in the making of a poem they have participated in a mystery, then they know that they have been admitted to a truth. A new generation of poets may not feel that they are members of a fellowship of dead poets, but when they read dead poets' work and see that they, too, have participated in mysteries, the living may feel that they are fellow-practitioners in a great calling.

Patricia McCarthy

Talking to the Dead

R.V. Bailey: *The Losing Game* (Mariscat Press, 2010)
Penelope Shuttle: *Sandgrain and Hourglass* (Bloodaxe Books, 2010)
Tim Liardet: *The Storm House* (Carcanet, 2011)
Gjertrud Schnackenberg: *Heavenly Questions* (Bloodaxe Books, 2011)

Poetry has always found broken hearts, and broken hearts have found poetry. Jonathan Bate is quoted at the very beginning of *The Losing Game* as saying: 'Without loss, there would be no reason for... poetry'. Some elegies are always there to prop one up in the face of death – such as Tennyson's 'In Memoriam', Rilke's 'Requiem', and Thomas Hardy's 1912-13 poems. The end of the twentieth century echoed with Douglas Dunn's *Elegies* to his wife (Faber, 1985), and Ted Hughes' bestselling *Birthday Letters* (Faber, 1998). The beginning of the twenty first century celebrated Christopher Reid's powerful elegies about the 'irreparable damage' of his vivacious wife's death in *A Scattering* (Areté Books, 2009), which won the Costa Book Prize, with its haunting analysis of bereavement stitched by 'Grief, the couturier' as Douglas Dunn named it. These keens or laments comprise, in part, eulogies; a resuscitation or resurrection of the dead person through memory and words. Specific realistic detail is often supplied, or there is the narration of, as Douglas Dunn defined, ' the legendary, retrospective fictions'. The past often becomes a sanctuary, as an attempt is made to come to terms with loss and also with the altered identity of the isolated bereft person.

In his moving fragment of an autobiography, *The Presence* (Vintage Books, 2008), which is both a record of personal grief – his wife, Joan, was killed in an accident in the car which the poet was actually driving – and a portrait of a loving marriage, Dannie Abse refuses to read a book given to him by a friend: Joan Didion's *The Year of Magical Thinking*, because it is about 'the mental illness of bereavement'. Indeed, all these collections prove that bereavement is no mental illness, but a vital process to be gone through by a fully living human being, until a necessary adjustment is reached, when, as Abse says, 'loneliness' can be changed to 'solitude'. Abse's beautiful little companion book to *The Presence* deserves a mention here: *Two for Joy: Scenes from Married Life* (Hutchinson, 2010). These finely-handled poems are celebratory, even if elegiac in tone because the past consisting of fifty years of a very successful loving marriage is Abse's sanctuary. It is interesting to note that Abse could handle the rush of his sudden bereavement only in prose.

It is hardly surprising that the language of grief used by different poets has cathartic similarities. For example, Bailey, Shuttle and Liardet all address the lost person intimately as 'you' which turns their poems into letters or a 'calling', even if they are formally written in poetic form and the addressee is not physically there to read them or to answer back. It is worth remembering here that TS Eliot said a good poet should be judged by his letters. All three poets also personify Grief, Sorrow and Sadness as allegorical figures. All four, including Gjertrud Schnackenberg, use repetition as a form of keening, as well as patterning, flashbacks, and speak to the ghosts of their lost loved ones; all focus at various stages on different kinds of metamorphosis; and show the shock disbelief, the difficulty of adjustment. All are powerful testaments to the bonding power of love in a close personal relationship cut short – whether of marriage, of a same-sex or filial relationship.

Elegies are as important for the reader as for the writer of them. Just as in attending a funeral, the person brings along all his/her experienced bereavements to date, so in reading elegies, the reader brings to the lines the emotion carried over from any past bereavements. In this way, the elegy expands and is the receptacle of a variety of mournings, even subconscious ones. Bailey and Reid write their haunting poems very soon after the deaths of their loved one. Their emotion is more raw than in the slightly more distant stage of grief expressed by Liardet who writes a year after his brother's mysterious death, and also by Shuttle who is on her second book of love and loss about her late husband, the poet Peter Redgrove. Schnackenberg's sequence, though seemingly immediate in its experience of death, could be written at any time in the mourning process, or even in the non-time constructed by the void that appears after loss.

Douglas Dunn in his *Elegies* states that he is 'dedicated to the one/ Pure elegy' proving the 'truth' of him and his wife ('us') as 'Particular, eternal'. U.A. Fanthorpe's long-term partner, R.V. Bailey, in *The Losing Game*, achieves precisely this. The modest little pamphlet of nineteen pages reflects Bailey's humility and does not prepare the reader for the especial accessible bigness and faultlessness of each of her impressive, assured poems. In these spare twelve poems, we see Bailey trying to cope with her suddenly enforced, single identity. She addresses U.A. Fathorpe in the vocative 'you', so that the reader feels privileged at being let into the confidential tones of grief while at the same time building up a daily picture of the very close loving relationship of the two distinct characters. The direct speech used frequently enables the reader to enter the lively reality of the two who spark it off, at times all the more movingly, with minor differences and fond annoyances, as Bailey relives their compatible times together. The first beautifully honed sonnet, which acts as a container for the emotion, uses broken lines, as in the final stanzas of Hardy's 'The Going', to show how broken up she is. It also initiates the role-swapping as Bailey grieves. Fanthorpe had a habit of losing things 'Distractedly. Maddeningly' and Bailey would reassure her that things would turn up. Now, however, 'In this losing game', it is she who needs to carry out the former 'ritual moves' of her partner, even to 'pray to St. Anthony of Padua', and to hunt everywhere: 'Maddeningly. Distractedly'. The last line of the octet is effectively reversed in the last line of the sestet and cleverly symbolises the role-reversal. It shows how she is in the process of actually becoming her partner which prolongs the two-in-one person that all lovers aim for even after Fanthorpe's death. But the very last line is full of despair: 'Can't find you anywhere'. This unadorned language with deceptively simple tender assertions prevails throughout and adds to the pathos. In 'Second-Hand', for example, she wears Fanthorpe's clothes: 'They fit me just as you did'. In doing so, she again becomes Fanthorpe whose disembodied ghost now she fills with her own living body. The double entendre of the last line: 'You leave me far behind' reinforces the loss as in 'Hands': 'We'll not lose touch' which comes at the end of a poem describing the forbidden, clandestine meetings early in their relationship when their 'hands met/ like fugitives'. She recalls sensuously Fanthorpe's 'generous hands', 'confiding hands', 'forgiving hands' and her 'private hand' in hers and feels still, despite the death, she is still holding her hand. Original extended metaphors also come into play such as 'Finals' where Bailey sits at the deathbed of her dying partner, not needed, 'irrelevant'. She imagines 'This is Schools, Finals, the last day/ Of the Tripos, the fatal minutes/ Ticking by'. Again she uses the direct speech of Fanthorpe 'if things were different' saying flippantly and reassuringly, 'Off with you love! Enjoy it all – / I'll see you later'. In the brilliant use of repetition of the obsessive 'You' in 'Parts of Speech', the poet tries to learn a new language: 'I, not *we*;/ My, not *our*' and the actual word '*you*' is what she is still in love with as forty years ago. The rhyming couplets in the final poem insist on them being a pair still. Love insists and persists, as in all these poems,

> Intimate as breath, loyal as a shadow, close as a cry.
> Nothing will shake it off.
>
> Nor should you try.

Penelope Shuttle's latest collection, *Sandgrain and Hourglass*, comes on the heels of her haunting *Redgrove's Wife*, published four years earlier. It demonstrates impressively how mourning does not stop necessarily quickly after the death of the loved one, but goes on and on. Here she has come to terms not so much with her husband's death which has left her carrying her heart around everywhere with her, 'wrapped in newspaper', 'such a lump, trailing blood', but with living with him differently as time modulates and re-shapes grief. She continues to talk to him in letter form and in the passionate, beautifully executed poem 'What I Want' she imagines being close to his new spirit existence in the natural universe wherein he seems to own 'daytime skies', nights, forests, which she wants him to wrap, fold and hide her in and to let her 'sway/ in that bright, winking maze of tears,/ for one hundred years'. She admits

> Last, best of all
> write me a letter, sweetheart,
> be sure to put in all the syntax,
> the verbs and the pronouns, that's all I ask,
>
> a single, grammatically correct love letter
> in your own weatherwise hand.

The process of mourning is not complete. They are 'so far apart, so conjoined' and this is what she has to settle for: conjuring his body and his language to keep him real before her. Although 'the vial of your heart/ so long our wellkept secret.// I can't bear to look there,/ even through closed eyes', it is as an aubergiste, a captain, a warrior, that she gazes with desire at all his intimate body parts, albeit in memory. The reader is almost an unwitting voyeur as she surveys his 'skin's familiar landmarks' and admits tragically: 'I yearn over the vineyard of you', trusting that 'love blindfolded is love still'. At times, however, she does try to understand how he exists differently, spatially and outside time and this links her tentatively to Schnackenberg who will be reviewed last. Though elsewhere Redgrove is her 'song-master' – as if still alive, in 'Looking Back' she does attempt to see him in the abstract: 'I know you drink from my sober glass/ as song drinks'. Likewise, in the delicately achieved poem 'Telling the Time' she shows how she has learnt how to view time not chronologically (like Schnackenberg):

> I tell time
> by the kingfisher's swoop above the river.
>
> I set my watch
> by the woodpecker's countdown to noon

The lyricism here adds to the poignancy, for her deceased husband has lost nature's beauties, while she clings onto them for comfort and continuance.

A similar insistence on the lyrical sustains her in 'The Scattering'. The carefully-patterned form is like a spell, with the deliberate biblical-sounding language of a succession of 'Be's: 'Be the mentor of cherry trees' or 'Be wild rose or hellebore or all-heal' adding a veneration to the process of scattering. Like Schnackenberg, Shuttle searches for words where there are no words and manages: 'Descend as a vein of silver,/ never to be seen,/ deep in the lynx-eyed earth// Rise as a barn owl white as dusk'.

In 'The Repose of Baghdad' Shuttle imagines all the places on earth where they have been together but won't be again although the pathos arises from the repeated pattern of the first conditional: 'If I ever' and 'You won't'. The negatives where he won't be ironically hint precisely at her lack of acceptance that she will never be with him again. In this poem she gives the reader a tour of ancient places in the east and west known to them as a couple. They form a kind of surrealistic collage which represents a makeshift afterlife in her head, somewhat similar to Schnackenberg's surrealistic odysseys in her collection.

In the strongest poems, she continues to talk to Redgrove as in her previous volume, but does extend her world, for example, to her father, Jack, to Edward Thomas, Faust, Francis Bacon. It could be said, however, that the deliberate levity in some of the poems strikes a discord with the intensely-felt elegies to her deceased husband, and the collection would have had greater impact, and been sufficient, had it been shorter. Matching Bailey's humility, and Bailey's 'Finals' with her poem 'Student', she disarmingly suggests in an equally extended metaphor that we are all students in grief. She personifies Grief as a demanding professor marking in red all her wrong answers in exercise book after exercise book as she prepares to take the final examination after long terms and very few holidays. 'Whatever dead language asks the questions' she feels she 'must graduate with honours/ from this sorrowful schoolroom// scrape a living by all I've learned so long and so hard'.

Learning is rife in all these collections. In *The Storm House*, Tim Liardet performs his own wide-reaching inquest on his brother's mysterious death, and the reader is induced throughout to find clues and to piece together what happened while the poet himself makes his harrowing discoveries, and draws his conclusions in the second reflective half of the book, consisting of 32 extremely well-honed sonnets. The subject matter is donné and no one would wish it on him/herself, but Liardet pulls off a genuine, agonisingly-won tour-de-force. The collection is very bravely written; nothing is spared, the tone never falters, yet the confrontation with his brother's difficulties and death show such compassion, such empathy that the shocking material never diminishes into bathos or sensational melodrama. Indeed, it is Liardet's quiet strength in dealing with his disturbed brother's murder of his woman, and his ensuing murder, with his brother's symbiotic relationship with his mother with whom he is always 'whispering and giggling', with the mother's mental decline into confusion and the father's death, with a weird picture of a 'Grandfather in Drag' that maximises the powerful impact of this taut, complex book.

The sequence as a whole is intricately interknit with repeated images such as craneflies, wire, snarl, nod, shrug, mirrors, glass, and different colours like little leifmotifs at intervals, stitching the whole traumatic fabric together, as well as reiterated phrases which echo like mantras through the book. Simple deliberate mantras for calming are there, too, like the poet in 'Grief-fugue' listening to the CD on mute that has a life of its own as it spins 'from sound-pulse to sound-pulse', mesmerising the poet who at the end whispers: *'play it again, play it again, play it again'* – a song familiar to the poet and to readers, without the 'Sam' at the end. There is the sympathetic, non-judgemental younger brother, the poet, who witnesses his brother ruining a party with his heavy drinking yet then leniently pictures him back home lying under the stars on the roof-tiles whispering: 'I know how to behave,/ I know how to behave, I know how to behave' – as if the difficult brother can't help himself. There is the strong bond of brotherhood, despite all the horror, at the crematorium in 'Lay Thee Down'. As in several of the poems on their childhood days together, Liardet fondly recalls when they both shared the back room and talked nonstop and he would always repeat: *'for the last time now goodnight, Davy;/ for the last time now goodnight, Davy'*. 'On Pett Level Beach' offers a monochrome photograph of a seemingly ordinary family at the seaside: his family, under 'a laden, post-war sky'. The only hint of any violence to come stirs in the final couplet where the sea 'smashes against the breakwater/ and the breakwater smashes against the sea'. In 'Sky Egg' Liardet's compassion for his displaced brother is very moving: 'Body and world were never the place/ for you to live in'. He pictures his brother climbing high up into the sky and himself being his brother's counterweight, the 'gravity' in his 'shoes'. He imagines his brother bringing down to safety not a bird's egg, but a 'sky egg', 'the rarest and most susceptible outer shell/ of life's longing for itself – so pristine and so sky blue', as he, the boy poet, shouts up to him with concern *'don't fall, don't fall'*. The juxtaposition at the end of the poem: 'Now you fall through time, if not through time and space' illuminates the frustrating sadness that the brother couldn't manage to live in this world. Innocent memories like these serve as a palimpsest over the horror and trauma of the main narrative. For example in 'The Constables Call', the poet wishes his brother had been able to explain what happened. Instead the constables' macabre focus is on the brother's 'dark and horny' toenails 'like the case' which continue to grow: 'they flourish like clues and curl back into accusation'. Finally the image becomes surrealistic: they resemble 'Nosferatu's/ fingernails scratching a name on the air'. In 'The Gorse Fires' the coroner speaks clinically about his inspection of bodies, some of which 'catch hold of the lies of the dead'.

Like Schnackenberg's *Heavenly Questions*, *The Storm House* recalls T.S. Eliot's *Four Quartets* in its musical structure, its devices of repetition, paradox, of images that evolve, turn back on themselves and change – in this case in a basically selfish universe 'whose every centre is/ a little pot of self-regard'. Startlingly original images abound such as: 'the mind's lampshade', 'a Galapagos of kickmarks' on his brother's face, 'deckchairs which blow themselves pregnant', a bronze cupid 'toupéed in stormflies' and 'a star in the cavity the pilot light keeps' demonstrating how, like Schnackenberg, Liardet succeeds in making domestic images cosmic. There are other subtle hints of *Four Quartets* (such as the clog-dance, see below), but Liardet makes the words his own, such as in sonnet 14 in the second section:

> There were many journeys, there were half journeys
> but that of the heart a pilgrimage in reverse,
> a return to the source from which to set out again.

In the second half of the book, a sequence of sonnets, Liardet's brother is still addressed throughout: 'Sequestered brother, a year dead, now the world/ must get by without you', 'Untalkative brother, a year dead, everywhere world/ is in the ascendant'. In sonnets 19 and 20 Liardet allows himself to imagine in graphic detail the blow his brother dealt to his woman 'on the fragile pot of her skull', and imagines her carrying 'the identical likeness' of him 'in her dying fall' during which 'she shed herself like a shawl'. What the poet is left with is, like the other elegists, 'the panic of not finding you anywhere' and the dialling tone of the telephone which has an ironic and almost sinister 'sing-song note at large in it' ever since his brother hung up on him and never spoke to him again.

The structure of the whole sequence is symmetrical, mathematically ingenious as the final thirty two sonnets reflect on the first part and mirror it cleverly, continuing the horror story yet the language is its own reprieve. In this final section the feeling is perhaps more disciplined, more retrospective, each sonnet built to contain the emotional weight that is so personal it becomes impersonal, each sonnet also delicately and subtly picking up images and themes from the first section which is in a variety of forms: tercets, couplets, free verse, long lines, short lines, occasional rhyme, half rhyme, slant rhyme comprising a jagged kind of music contrasting with the full orchestra of sonnets in the second half. Here in one of the final sonnets, Liardet actually defines the music:

> now that I must see for two, I must attempt also
> to live the life I owe you and find a way to clog-dance,
> to jitterbug, to tap or otherwise to jig
> on the brilliant ice that is your coffin lid.

He continues: 'Imagine it all, brother, set to such music'. And indeed, Liardet, the virtuoso, manages throughout to accomplish what he imagines for his brother: 'the music, the events, glancing off each other'.

The Storm House might be an uncomfortable read in its relentless intensity, but it is unique in its courageous exposition – through perfectly achieved poetry – of what it means to belong to the family of a man who is both a murderer and murdered.

Liardet resembles Gjertrud Schnackenberg in his music, and in his surrealistic images such as in the poem about the rubbish his brother kept in his pockets, he imagines his metamorphosis, or 'reinvention' into 'open cigarette pack for jaw,/ say, a mark-up price for one eye and bottle cap/ for the other, crushed tampon for a nose;// a torn-off half of strap-line for mouth'. He is also similar to her in the breadth of his vision and in his careful choice of references that have multiple, relevant meanings in his text: Nosferatu, Rasputin, Festé, the Batalha Christ, Ugolino who has the longest single speech of the damned in Canto 33 of Dante's *Inferno*, Dostoyevsky's Raskolinov, the protagonist of *Crime and Punishment* who kills for his own sake, Tchaikovsky's 'Death of Ivan Ilyich', from Tolstoy, a man who wasted his own life and could not imagine his own death ('Ilyich's violins' referring to Tchaikovsky's famous Violin Concerto in D major, Op. 35). Paralleling Schnackenberg's quest to make sense of other worlds are Liardet's attempts, too, to define his brother on the other side of life, particularly in the final two sonnets of *The Storm House*' where his brother might be 'a single *ohm*/ in that rip of lightning' or 'every decibel/ that cracks open and throws seeds', might know 'the turnings beyond the world/ that have never been mapped'.

The American poetess, Gjertrud Schnackenberg, is a startling find. *Heavenly Questions* is certainly a highly ambitious major opus not only for our time but for all time, brimming with the poet's own learning and also offering its learning to readers to interpret according to their own capacity. The three very brief introductory notes to the work help the reader negotiate the text. 'The Heavenly Questions', we are told, is a translation from the ancient poem, 'Tianwen' by Qu Yan (c.340-278 B.C.E.) which consists of a series of unanswerable, cosmological, philosophical and mythological questions which, according to a legend from the second century C.E., the banished poet wrote on the walls of temples during his wanderings. She is also inspired by two ancient legends about the Hagia Sophia building in Turkey – that the Imperial Door was made of wood from Noah's ark, and a seventeenth century Turkish legend that the hundreds of doors of the Hagia Sophia could not be counted accurately because they were under a magic spell.

Even in her earlier substantial volume, *Supernatural Love: Poems 1976-2000* (Bloodaxe, 2001), in which she demonstrates how alive her poems are on the page, how well researched they are, myths made her own and how she is a genuine storyteller, she writes: 'You believed/We intuit the sound of the spheres, Dante,/ When God touches our ears. *Ephphatha. Be thou opened*'. Here she has sewn the seeds of intuiting the spheres in *Heavenly Questions*. The chessboard too is there: 'Through the doorway/ The kitchen floor squares make a chessboard/ Whose figures have crumbled/ To small heaps of dust'. This becomes a major extended metaphor in *Heavenly Questions* and mirrors, along with all the other mirroring – as in Liardet's *Storm House* – our own living game as mortals on this earth.

It is interesting to note that, not only Liardet, but Schnackenberg uses this same device of repetition of sentences or phrases like mantras which appear and re-appear slightly altered throughout the sequence and each individual poem, but with a resonance that holds the various parts together. In the first of the two lullabies, for example, 'Archimedes Lullaby', the comforting sound 'And hush now, all is well now, close your eyes' recalls the rocking of cradles and also of course Dame Julian of Norwich. This is companioned by: 'And all in play, with everything in play'. The play theme, mixed in with the mathematical abstract shapes – 'a sphere inscribed within a cylinder', ratios, square roots, diagrams, angles and weights (the latter as in Liardet) and weightlessness which try to define infinities, illustrate our limited human need to define: 'It never ends, this dire need to know', to ascertain where everything begins to (another mantra) 'Materialize, and dematerialize'. In the second lullaby, further on in the sequence, the same 'hush now' and 'play' mantras appear, even if with slightly altered word order. The mantras everywhere such as 'but never mind', 'the house where no beloved ever dies' which is hauntingly sought for, the desperate 'just say he'll live' (on the ward), 'no questions now', the urgent 'O say not so' which becomes an even more urgent Buddhist exhortation: 'O say not so, Ananda, say not so', as well as the humble repeated plea: 'O beggar' plus the 'begging hand' are memorable and constitute the keening chord of the work.

Divided into six long poems, neither of which is separate, but integral to the whole, the sequence is both a passionate love poem and an elegy, alternating fluently between the lyric and the epic. The rhythmical, steady thump of the blank verse recalls Milton and ironically mimics a regular heartbeat, although the heart of her beloved in the course of the sequence stops. In fact, the book takes off where Eliot's *Four Quartets* ends and in her own individual, erudite voice in perfect pitch, Schnackenberg achieves a tremendously moving poetic, in places dramatic, treatise on death, both personal and universal, on a possible or not possible after-life, on history, the future, on time itself, and on universes behind universes. With intellectual, technical and aesthetic innovation, she skilfully weaves Christianity, Buddhism, Hinduism, eastern and materialist philosophies, quantum physics, geology, anatomy, the Gnostics, mystics and much more around the death of her 'beloved'. The past, the future and the present all become, as in J.B. Priestley, no time, or all the tenses happening at once, outside man-made chronology – 'all self-creating time/ Evaporated'. The text is dotted with classical and literary allusions as she attempts to solve 'riddles' or 'Heavenly Questions' such as 'all those being-riddles' which 'lay unsolved', 'the 'being-riddle buried in a story' – and such a story or stories in which 'the teller and the listener were one'.

The microcosm of the actual ward is mirrored, along with all the other mirror images, in the macrocosm conjured in her stream of consciousness in which she herself seems to mirror her beloved's narcotic-induced delirium in which she takes the reader on a Homeric-style odyssey. She hints just this: that she gets inside his mind: 'phantom images inside/ Another's mind dissolve inside one's own', and 'Opiates. The ship of Theseus/ Passing above. A water ceiling sways'/ The masts broken, torn down, no one aboard'. This recalls, by chance, Christopher Reid imagining his wife's hospice bed is a little boat rocking to the 'lullaby-barcarolle' made up from the 'ragbag repertoire/ of songs she loved to sing'. Reid's odyssey, however, lasts only a few lines, cut short by her only too real fit: 'Only in that space/ of the mind where the wilful/ metaphors thrive/ has it now pushed/ out into the open sea/ and begun to travel/ beyond time and place/ never to arrive'. Schnackenberg's odyssey expands to include pictures of other earths and seas, full of geological details such as rifts and plates, water-ceilings, spirals and waves, as well as worlds backwards and forwards in time, of Ming dynasties, Tamburlaine, Scheherazade, of Genghis Khan, of Balkan wars and Afghanistan, of cities such as 'Baghdad, Aleppo, Cairo, Samarkand', of phantom battlefields despite the fact that 'everything that ever happened fades', and *What makes the indivisible divide?*', of walls made of air, invisible walls, walls of the heart, of the Byzantine labyrinth that perhaps construct the only house possible 'where the beloved never dies'. Here, too, are abstract shapes, helixes, cusps, spires, whorls – so gifted is Schnackenberg at conjuring the language of geometrical abstractions – where maybe the dying beloved can find a 'nonself' or even be 'unborn'.

The text is regularly brought down to earth, as it were, by a series of flashbacks to the hospital or to intimate memories shared with her beloved as, on behalf of all humanity, she endeavours to make sense of his/our mortality. These are full of exclamatory regrets, hopes too soon dashed ('But let him live') in the specifically framed and shrunken world of the hospital ward with its lift, the surgeon and the nurse. The narrative in the flashbacks as her beloved experiences his last days and moments, then finally dies, is both harrowing, intimate and tender. As the persona, presumably the poet, keeps vigil at the bedside of her dying beloved, their 'hands entwined', she is aware that 'a ring of useless keys/ had fallen from my hand, but never mind'. Despite her hope that 'he would live', 'Just say he'll live' if a door opened, *The Heavenly Questions'* were 'raving on the wall/ Were half-dissolved, were mere graffiti now'. This leads to the metaphysical question: can we make sense of an '*unbidden universe*' if we ourselves are '*unbidden*'? As she tries to reassure herself that he will live: 'It seems a shadow knife/Was cutting shadow flesh, but never mind'. This knife, it turns out, is 'Handleless' and 'without a blade', pointing to the impossibility of a cure. Nevertheless, his body still lives as 'Beloved body's beauty, lying still,/ His hand silk to my lips, no questions now', and, later, 'Our hands entwined: a single heart drained white'. The intimate tenderness is heart-wrenching every time we are brought back to her at his bedside, even if he becomes a mere 'blurry shadow on a scan'. The nurse's bogus reassurance of 'he's doing fine' as he has nil by mouth is an ironic contrast to the genuine reassurance in the poet/persona's exploratory visions. The anatomical cutting open leads to the idea of the 'uncuttable' atoms, 'The indivisibles', and the mortal body comes under scrutiny:

> An image no one made, or made by God,
> Or self-made, self-dissolving, self-aware.
> Who then, or what, hallucinated this?

This is juxtaposed with the healthy times they enjoyed together written in the form of a beautiful, almost Shakespearian eulogy (as is the way with some of the elegies already discussed) giving him heroic qualities. It also serves as a living, sensuous portrait of her beloved as a gentle, magnetic, understanding, passionate man, 'master of his heart, and of himself', capable of 'voluptuous surrender'. This eulogy is kept to herself, repeatedly prefaced by 'How could I say', the aim of their union which transcended the daily: 'To find each other's spirit's melting point/ And changing states, never such nakedness/ Between such two.'

Her language, as he dies, is reminiscent of *Antony and Cleopatra* in its tragic intensity, and even in the images that she applies to herself and to her dying lover – such as being each other's 'conqueror'. Excruciatingly moving are her words: 'I held him like a passion-tattered cloak', and as she conjures for herself, and for her dead beloved, a mantra 'Forever rest', 'Forever, ever rest', and as she draws her hand away from his, her utterance 'Let nothing evermore be dear to me' could well be the words of other elegists in the grips of loss. Her helplessness would be understood too: 'I swayed, dead on my feet among the living', 'But couldn't draw one breath on his behalf/ Nor add a single heartbeat to his life'.

The Hagia Sophia building inspires all the door images in the sequence. The door of the ward itself changes: 'The door I crazed with knocking reappeared./ A transitory door, lit on the wall,/ Drenched radiant orange, ablaze beyond the bed,/ A milli-millimeter depth of red,/ Painted in a nearby universe'. This door magnifies and multiplies into countless different doors 'sunset-painted', 'the door to the house where no one ever died', an invisible door, a door 'bolted shut the same as left ajar' (paradoxes abound), a demolished door, 'doors that multiply and multiply', an added door to the tally of doors, doors 'torn from their ancient hinges', phantom doors, and towards the end the shocked 'cabinet doors jarred open on the sight/ Of mirror-image towers, moving off,/ A chess set sprawled'... 'A war/ Evaporated', 'The nameless battles surging through a maze/ had vanished'.

> A thousand nights of play had disappeared
> As if the thousand nights had never been.

It seems, therefore, that all these doors are doors of some kind of perception and it is only towards the end of the sequence, culminating in the disintegration of the chess set that has been predominant as an image throughout, that chronological time has been overcome, with 'untold tales/ Of battles never fought and unlived lives/And useless squares for legendary wars/ that never happened, deaths that no one died.' Lord Krishna, who sets out the pawns again and continues to play chess, has said, despite dramatic expectations based on the battles in the Mahabharata, that he cannot bring an end to wars, and concludes sagely:

> There are no slayers here, there are no slain.
> The conquered and the conqueror are one.

And a little later, carrying the pervasive and perhaps only redeeming message of the whole sequence:

> I am the same to all, Lord Krishna said.
> To all beings my love is ever one.

Writing is a theme throughout, presumably linking to the ancient banished Chinese poet, Qu Yuan, as well as to the poet/persona who writes with a soft Venus pencil which takes on a life of its own and 'gives up on us'. Her paper thins, becomes a tablet; there are pages that turn and can't be turned; the pencil point even 'hallucinates' like both herself and her dying beloved; the paper becomes pulp, ashes, turns into

> A mystical directory of the living,
> Each page a random sample of Creation
> And changing version of the Book of Life

In this directory she finds her beloved's name 'still listed with the living/ Whose stories vanish, leaving only names/ Recycled and reused'. She imagines also a shell's scroll being written on by 'underwater ink' 'with wondrous deeds' and the 'remnants of/ a Heavenly Question, lightly brushed across/ With opalescent ore of consciousness'. Ultimately an unread book lies on her lap, its author the god of writers that analyses war and gives Krishna the last voice in the sequence. Annihilation approaches and here 'the god of writers broke his pen', perhaps a bleak vision of a universe where words ultimately fail and whatever is is not.

Schnackenberg speaks on behalf of all the elegists discussed here when she asks: 'What were the words I tried to cast a spell/ To understand?' Bailey, Shuttle, Liardet and Schnackenberg, plus the elegists mentioned, all cast their own especial spells in trying to understand life, death and loss. Liardet, too, speaks for them all:

> Talking to the dead's not easy. I'm robbed in daylight
> of the gift of speech – any mouthful of words
> as if cluttered out with stones impervious
> to the seep of listening

Shakespeare knew this when, at the death of Cordelia, he gave Lear these words:

> Howl, howl, howl! O, you are men of stones;
> Had I your tongues and eyes, I'd use them so
> That heaven's vaults should crack.

How thankful we can be, then, that these elegists, with their 'gifts of speech' do get past the stones, to give the vaults of heaven a resounding crack!

Lyn Moir

Guggenheim Swans

Stolid pilgrims might have shown surprise
at silver swans disporting on the shore,
but never disbelief –

a sign from heaven, a miracle
to speed already calloused feet
west and west again,
leaving behind the devils of the sea.

A pause to drink, to offer prayers
to la Begoña on her hill,
a glance behind
and then away

along the coast
past Altamira's lurking bison herd,
or inland, drawn to merge
thin trickles of men
in the river of westing souls.

The silver swans were always there,
unseen,
great feathered arcs, time-frayed,
now tinted tungsten wings
attracting pilgrims of their own.

Climate change: after a drought
arroyos dry for centuries
flood again, torrents of pilgrims
in search of what they can.

Train from Aranjuéz

As we approach Madrid,
railway tracks fan out,
a holding pen
for superannuated stock.

The skeletons of ancient carriages,
predating our war, perhaps even theirs,
their faded paint suggesting fabled names:

Atocha, Chamartín,
Carabanchel,
Valencia, Cuenca,
Teruel...

each place-name brings six dozen faces,
gap-toothed, grinning,
peering through the slats,
cigarettes dangling from dusty lips,
hoarse cheers fading in the sun.

The carriages are peeling prisons, dry,
so frail a bird could splinter them,
their wheels a miracle of rust.

M.H. Miles

August

Dry, dusty, motionless month
Plaited with muddled memory
Of love and hope and gentle death.

Chain Mail

Dull-lit metal houses, glimpsed through
Tin-trunk trees twisting skywards.
Doors open.
Grey, bent figures trudge through the half light
To iron factories, slate schools.
Hear silenced news and wanton pedagogy.
Watch screaming sirens stifling nihilism.
See burning bodies turn to molten lead.
Tick-tack rain jangles the chain-mail leaves
As we stumble, in the half light.

The Flats

Her voice, her hand, you loved then
As you walked the flats to be
By the sand dunes and the tufted grass
To watch the seeping sea.

A world you owned and loved then
Cycling, free, beside the dykes;
The big, wide sky, the North Sea breeze
And log-fired winter nights.

But that woman whom you loved then
Your expectation dulled.
The soft-gloved grip superfluous,
Her hopes for you annulled.

Abegail Morley

Place

I want to clear a space
like 4pm clears a school yard,
exhales its children, to leave
itself blank for the holidays.

I take a short cut over grass,
race across netball courts
scraping up fragments of your life
with a fine toothed comb -

a litter of gifts, (a hair slide,
a compass, a multi-purpose pencil).
There is a deficiency in loss,
it cannot be found

shouting round playgrounds,
jumping over a fence,
or wondering how high to lift it
to roll through thistles.

But even in this field
there is not enough space to hold you.
Even with the sky drawn back
and the clouds pushing around its edge,

distance and foreground
wrap you, their eyes once like ice
now melt at your name.

Nigel Holt

Eldorado

'Is it indeed so? If I lay here dead,
Wouldst thou miss any life in losing mine?
                Elizabeth Barrett Browning: Sonnet XXIII, *Sonnets from the Portuguese*

Tomorrow Luis will come early.
Tomorrow Luis will start the garden
tasks; tame the wildness
I have watched grow each day through
the glass; grow thick in fat, slow shoots;
squeeze out life in tight green coils;
want ingress to the parlour and the hall
– let me in to the *Postamt* and the *Küche*.

'Wherever a joyous bird sings,
he sings for another.'

Tomorrow Luis will come;
will cut the grass; move the plants
that multiply in murmuring corners
and turn their sallow faces to me;
rake the border so they will not pass
the line drawn out upon the earth.

'Wherever a tiny star twinkles far away,
it twinkles for another.'

Tomorrow Luis will come early
so I may pick the bushes clean;
so I may yet taste again the blush
of berry flesh beneath the tongue:
a twin dessert of sweet and ripeness in old age
 – that I stab my fingers on their wiry barbs
adds pleasure to the profit of their blood.

Tomorrow. Tomorrow Luis will come early;
he will come to lighten darkness in the house.
For after all the jobs are done, and fires of dead
leaves are lit and left to burn, their ash disperses.
And, in the lush shade of the *Telefüncken*,
the Winter Games give way to Disney
and Disney to despair, as he bids good night.

Tomorrow, Luis will come early:
tomorrow – he will come.

The first line is translated from a recently found letter written by Josef Mengele in Sao Paolo, Brazil, dated, February 1976.
Lines 10 and 18 are also from Josef Mengele's diary (details from *Der Spiegel*)

D.W. Brydon

Shells

i

I stand before the violent sea,
watch as it throws up
kelp, a starfish, a scarf.

The night recedes to morning and false joy
like the first Christmas after their divorce.
The sun strews tinsel on the waves.

ii

My father once held a shell to my ear
bringing the far cry of a seagull
wheeling round and round.

Now everything is amplified. Calls of
seven gulls reverberate
as the rescue boat ploughs back.

In the wake
the noises will grow louder:
radiator creak, fridge hum, clock tick.

When the day finally comes,
I will not hear the vicar's words
encase my father.

James Roberts

The Graveyard of Little St David's

This circle of carved rocks
once dedicated to the dead,
dissolves.

Stones lean into shadowed air,
falling through centuries.
Rain smoothes the chiselled graves
leaving faint molten forms
on their blank surfaces.
The names of the dead
drip underground: Thomas, Morgan, Hughes.
Yew roots reach through bones
to where spent rain trickles;
they wrench down, drink,
streams flow backwards into air.
And each drop of dark water
holds a grain of sandstone
filling each green needle
with a fragment of a name.

Tim Murdoch

The Ancestral Imperative

For PRM 1908-1993

I was told it was essential to grieve –
that even before you left, grief
was waiting in the wings disguised
in mild manners and lackadaisical pursuits

or as fear – as a dog getting set to bite –
and I was told, until I grieved, nothing
could be resolved... yet none of this
sounded authentic, there seemed no point

in leaving you behind – on the contrary
the important quest was to take you along
with me on this scenic ride, enjoying
all the things your martyred self refused;

was to redeem the highlight – or shadow
the long war years draped over your life
like when your West End show had to close
and you became a mother three times over

while bombs were falling, friends fighting.
In the aftermath you heroically failed
to acclimatise passively to suburbia,
join the golf club or die playing bridge.

So now I've opened wide and taken you in,
integrated you – no need to discuss it –
our common duty the search for meaning
uninterrupted by polite conversation.

You're essential to my self, such as it is.
I refuse to fragment it into now and then –
so go ahead, live anew and I will write
these lines in your presence, my absence.

Green Man Blues

His pasture's in chaos, uncultivated –
hedge-fruits enervating – the bitter, the sweet.
No Virgilian Eclogues, no bosom friendship
on offer, he turns back from paradise
reminding you why you're not there...

All he impishly reveals are your errors
of thought – the fear, the fatal hesitancy –
never pretending there are higher worlds
of attainment, merely ponting out
the dreary logic, dread authority, of this one.

Why would you put yourself through this
when you could find comfort elsewhere –
someone to tell you how well you're doing?
He's shown the humour in this one too, smiling
at your frantic progression to nowhere...

though not forsaking you – staying close
as if nothing else mattered to him
but your wakening in the dark forest,
walking with him out into the sunlight,
your true face taking shape through the leaves.

Peter Rawlings

Living in the Dark

Once dark was a novelty.
It came at the end of obscure station platforms
or down festering alleyways.
It was always brief in the city
lit up like a fairground.

But dark from four in the hills.
In need of fire this long night
with wind dashing all upright things.
Stoking the flames.
Watching candles flicker.
I try bright lucid Haydn
to fend off a black solid as coalface.

It is the time for inwardness.
Take in dense food.
Prepare for natural disasters.
The wind is working itself up.
Earlier in the uncertain light
I saw the fields strewn with flurries
and magpie and crow trying the east wind.
And yesterday lower down I saw a big branch of a beech
ripped from its trunk as an omen.

I used to dream of this,
in isolation, nature all round and closing in,
I alone to fend it off and survive.
I could almost prefer darkness.
I could be a mole.

But now it is a state of mind,
a condition like the task of living,
unrelenting as the winds.

The mind is made dark too.
I hear it outside myself calling for grace.
My thoughts are tested by the somnolent house
shaken awake by nature.

The mind under siege
does not know which way to go.

The Apple Room

And I thought his room would please the willing mind,
be a site of unnameable wonders,
perhaps the source of an explanation.
It would drench me in true values.

Then I saw it, bare as a Nissen hut,
chairless, mattress thrown on the floor,
a tangle of duvet in a flowery cover, pilling,
and a reek of feet.

I understood that place and person
were divided like past and future,
dry seed and ripe fruit, but such nurture
for such nature seemed like something broken.

Daily this poor cell sent him out
free of all the routine entrapments -
possessions cherished, objects shown like trophies,
colours to flatter, clothes of self-love.

It is where he had his being,
took the course of his years
in dreams, secret plans, in voluptuous solitude.
It is where he invented his gentle manners.

And he was for his time
unchallenged king of apples.
Malus, glossy malus.
Fragrant apple blossom,
burnished into bloom by sun and wind.
Fillingham Pippin, Acklam Russet, Tresillian Seedling,
Worcester Pearmain, Spartan.
Flecked apples were rosy to his face,
his crisp bite brightened his teeth.
He maintained a stockpile against
the dire end of fertility
and some are extant still in these afterdays,
inside the doomed room,
dulled in the old cracked bowl,
withered dry as death.

Sarah Ruden

King David Refuses to Mourn His Son

2 Samuel 12:20-23

I'm dressed. The sky is stone, my path a sea.
I'm going to him, he won't return to me.

I eat. The stony waves have stilled the sea.
I'm going to him, he won't return to me.

I worship, sowing grain across the sea.
I'm going to him, he won't return to me.

Sue Roe

Her Little Gloves

my father sees no point in anything
he opens the white cupboard in the hall
sees 'her little gloves'
it is full to bursting
it all comes bursting out of him

her boots, her little gloves on top of his …
I know what else comes pouring out like water
incredibly, her yellow legs, like nylon
shoulders thin as hangers
her words when they moved her, 'they will care for me'

her little gloves come catapulting out,
like missiles, hit the far wall that is me
water pours from my father, his shoulders shake
I don't want this, don't want to be hit in the face
by her gloves catapulting from their place

yesterday, it took him half an hour
to scrape the ice and snow from his frozen car
lift the hatch and slide his cello in,
drive the fifteen miles to try to play
music that means nothing any more

but I am thankful for this snowy image
him scraping the ice, sliding the cello in
his fingers on the strings, making the music
that meant the world to him, that was his world
before she said, 'and you shall have my rings'

Jackie Wills

Woman's legs as path

On the way back,
a blue garden is squashed
between tenements.

She stops you here.
Feel the pebble she fits
between each of your toes.

Her shins are ravines
climbers rope their way across.
Her skin is seasoned with salt, piss
and traces of myrtle.

Woman's head as jug

Today she pours the Water of Life – green
walnuts picked in June, beaten with a pestle.

Tomorrow, Melancholy Water tasting of gillyflower,
damask rose, musk and gold leaf.

She steeps pounds of rue for Plague Water,
and to clear *'mists and clouds of the head'*

infuses peacock dung and bruised millipedes
in spirit of lavender. Bending over a bowl

she might empty a reservoir, reveal the valley
it invaded. Her head is fired from the same earth.

Don Avery

The Egg-Room

Again she takes her cue, and Mabel smiles
at mention of the egg-room. 'Can you keep
a secret?' 'Good. With Father fast asleep,
I'd go to dances; sometimes walking miles
to meet the boys. We lived above the Store
and egg-room was below us, out the back.
At six o'clock he'd fetch me eggs to crack
and never notice I'd just swept that floor!'

Bed-ridden mostly, spoon-fed by another
and starting now to wander in her mind,
I pray she never asks me 'Who are you?'
But she is happy now at Rainbow View,
where all the nurses have been very kind.
I give them little gifts. As if from Mother.

William Francis

'Would you like to see her?'

Burrowed deep in bedclothes,
with her nose towards the wall

I want to raise my voice
Shake her gently till she wakes.
Do they know how deaf she is,
how loud you have to call –
how long it takes?

The nurse has combed her hair.
A ploughed field in the moonlight bright with snow
Cold as silk to finger-backs
The hard surprising heaviness
of frozen earth below.

Unthinkable to fold the stiff
white sheets back from her face.
Best leave her in a close embrace -
the tight hold of her little nest of linen.

The shadow that my body casts
moves fast across the landscape
of her shoulders, back and hips.

Turn out the light.
Give her undemanding night.
I lean to touch her forehead with my lips.

Dylan Willoughby

Annwn

Here, I happened upon the afterworld
Creviced behind Ffynone falls
As I wandered alongside the Dulas
A spectre from the before life

You met me there, nonchalant as the dead
Can sometimes be, you startled me
With a stillness we don't yet possess
And I didn't recognize you

I thought you might bargain for an exchange
Another year in my shoes
While I got to see what I was in for
But you weren't hungry for this place

Haunting's something the living invent,
You said, no need to reminisce
About betrayals and loss and loss
How I longed to see you again, I said

You were cool but not unkind in your goodbye
I closed my eyes before you left,
Not wanting to remember you vanishing
Twice. I stood by the broken pool.

Charles Baudelaire

I Give You These Lines

Translated by Jan Owen

I give you these lines so if my name should find
a port by chance in some far distant time,
and cause, at dusk, tomorrow's men to dream,
then, like a ship blessed with a strong north wind,

your memory shall survive, an old refrain,
tiring the reader like a cimbalom,
for I have linked you here to every rhyme
as part of our fraternal mystic chain.

From the heights of heaven to the lowest depths of hell
only I respond to you, cursed soul.
Transient as a passing shade, you tread

light-foot, serene, over the foolish ones
who will not see, who judge you bitter and hard,
jet-eyed statue, angel with brow of bronze.

Translation of *Je te donne ces vers afin que si mon nom*

Meditation

Translated by Jan Owen

Be a good child, my Sadness, settle down.
You've longed for evening – look, at last it's here:
the air's grown darker, gathering up the town,
with peace for some, for others, pain and fear.

Now, while the frantic mobs of mortal men
go chasing after remorse, the usual show
whipped on by pitiless pleasure, merciless fun,
give me your hand, my Sadness, together we'll go

far from them all. See how the dead years lean
from their balcony sky, in garments quaint and worn;
regret's faint smile is lifting along the west

where the dying sun drops under an arch and down,
and, like a long shroud trailing towards the east,
– listen, child, footsteps – sweet night's coming on.

Translation of *Recueillement*

Sergey Pantsirev

All Said

Translated by Richard McKane

All said. Don't extend the quote,
behind it, inevitably, is emptiness.
The definition of a clean page is more honest
than lines that have reached their addressee.

All said. You must realise I'm too tired
to search for words, forgotten in time
sometime, to which we'll never
return. Truth is simple:

all said, the rest is lies
there's only one form of epilogue.
All's left is to linger by the doorstep

and anxiously listen in to the night,
where our last rain dies down
with the unrepeatable echo of a dialogue.

Roald Mandelstam

Dance of Shades

Translated by Richard McKane

In Memory of V. Prelovsky

Quiet and clever
the touch-me-not shades
are dancing in the moonnight
in the middle of the road.

All the alarmed words
are flooded with wine,
the cautious shades
droop under the window.

Like a weeping birch,
a ringing pine
in starry autumn
or early spring –

wound in swaddling clothes
of lacy dances,
all that's long forgotten
comes alive again.

It's impossible not to be sad
in the shaky twilight,
dead friends
are like unforgettable dreams –

quick and clever,
touch-me-not shades
are dancing in the moonnight
in the middle of the road.

Roald Mandelstam (1932-1961) was not related to his famous namesake Osip Mandelstam. His father Charles who was sent to a camp in Uzbekistan in 1936, knew his poetry and that of Akhmatova, Pasternak and Tsvetaeva by heart. Roald had acute asthma from the age of four and later was to develop tuberculosis of the lungs then bones. Kiril Medvedev wrote for the fulsome Limbakh Collection: 'The poems of Roald Mandelstam are hostile to the establishment and sense his own feeling of being doomed and of the élite at the same time. In him there is a triumph of magic and master-craftsamanship'.

W S Milne

'Unknown modes of being': Geoffrey Hill's Late Poetry

Geoffrey Hill: *Oraclau* (Clutag Press, 2010)
Geoffrey Hill: *Clavics* (Enitharmon Press, 2011)

In *Oraclau*[1] we are introduced to Old Testament prophets (Enoch, who was immortal, Ezekiel, who had a vision of a new Temple), 'Great princes of the word,' the 'guardian Spirits,' 'Great sentinels of light,' the Welsh Bards – especially Taliesin, who, like Eliot's Tiresias, sees everything walking between two worlds. 'Orare' is to speak, as in wise counsellors interpreting signs, speaking the words of the god, or as in Hopkins's 'Sibylline Oracles' deciphering supernatural enigmas – 'Lord Apollo, / Bestower of conundrums' as Hill expresses it at one point in *Clavics*. So it is that Hill, the belated Delphian, speaks of 'a Welsh *apocalypse,*' as David Jones did of an '*Anathemata,*' a lifting of the veil, a revelation, a disclosure of something hidden, or the exaltation of a subject to a divine level – and in the process praises, as a self-confessed 'outsider,' Wales's 'unrivalled language.'[2] The tone of the poem is mainly elegiac, a midrash, as in Sidney Keyes' 'the high / Persons and lovely voices we have lost,' or 'I try to remember how it was / When leaves sang like finches and the Word / Was music.' The power of the oracle, or of the prophet, in Hill's dispensation, is severely limited in the contemporary world. This loss of the poet's status in society has long been a favoured theme of Hill's, but here the subject comes to fruition. The loss of the bardic voice means that we have foregone 'God's / grammar, as the poets once construed it.'

---

[1] In recent interviews Hill informs us that the book forms part three of an on-going sequence called *The Daybooks*, the title of which is reminiscent of Beethoven's *Tagebuch*, a diary the composer kept late in life. (The title is also reminiscent of Robert Lowell's last book of poems, *Day by Day*, 1977. Hill wrote a very detailed essay-review on Lowell's poetry in *Essays in Criticism*, April 1963.) The sequence comprises: *Al Tempo de 'Tremuoti, Odi Barbare, Oraclau, Clavics,* and *Familiar Epistles*. The five volumes will constitute the final section of Hill's *Collected Poems 1952-2012*, scheduled for publication by Oxford University Press in 2013.

[2] Hill's interest in Wales has more than a family aspect to it. In an interview in *Poetry Wales* of Summer 2010, he explains that he has 'a historical, theological, sociological and economic interest in what has happened to Wales,' and in his essay on the poetry of R. S. Thomas writes of 'a keen sense of fellow feeling' with the Welsh poet, and of 'a shared belief in the reality of original sin.' These last concerns are hardly new to Hill, but the concentration on Wales is. W. Gwyn Thomas reviewed *Oraclau* favourably in *The Guardian*, October 16, 2010, as did Damian Walford Davies in the 2010 Christmas Issue of *The Times Literary Supplement*. On 'apocalypse' see Ezra Pound's interview in *The Paris Review* with Donald Hall (1962): 'It is difficult to write a paradiso when all the superficial indications are that you ought to write an apocalypse.'

Let's look at *Oraclau* in detail. In the opening pages the poet tells us he is 'at the natures of things.'[3] By this he means that all things are elemented in Christ, and that all oracles fail before 'the living Oracle' of Christ Himself. Chiasmus is the technical key to the poem's structure (in Christian poetry the cruciform 'chiasmus' often represents Christ). The stanza-form is Spenserian, (and akin to Donne's 'A Litany' and 'A Nocturnal upon St. Lucy's Day'). Here we have a 'gross' of poems overthrowing the European 'metric' system (Hill is keen on his jokes). He has a nine-foot line to Spenser's six (a new metre in English, I think) which accounts for the poem's rugged musicality. These are 'the nine-foot seams' he labours at and extracts, adopting Welsh poetic intricacies.[4] There are four different rhyme-schemes with variants of half-rhyme and off-rhyme. The section where Humpty Dumpty is introduced is the only part of the poem where he employs a fifth rhyme-scheme (so it can't be put back together again, I suppose!) The fifth line of each stanza is the cross-over point. It is 'a crossed question' as he calls it ('crossing rhyme' in *Clavics*), 'the mathematics of the cross,' an 'acrostic' – a crossed stick– where 'the grand suspensions' meet, in the foundation-stone, the root-ground of all belief, in The Cross itself ('this axle-tree' as he calls it in *Clavics*, echoing Eliot of the *Four Quartets*).[5] With the possible exception of Shakespeare's *Sonnets*, substantive numerology is unusual in English poetry ('Numerology also makes much sense' Hill writes in *Clavics*, possibly thinking of Dante's poetry there). As I read it, the first four lines of each stanza are emblematic of transcendence, the last four of the sublunary realm, and the middle representative of 'the interchange / of life with death,' 'this intersection by the spiritual' with 'our mortal existence.' The majority of sections have the first four lines patterning ABBA, which is clearly God the Father, but then

---

[3] Note the use of the plural: the radical individuality of *things*, as in Hopkins' Scotistic theory of inscape. T. S. Eliot in his PhD thesis on F. H. Bradley writes of 'the subject's essential nature.' 'Essence' for Hill is Bradley's 'eternal intensity,' 'a spirit that divines the source.' So it is that Hill's poetry abounds with angels (one has only to look at the cover of his *Collected Poems* to see how important they are to him). In *Oraclau* he talks of 'Felled angelism,' and the sub-heading to his essay 'Style and Faith' is a quotation from Benjamin Whichcote: 'If it were not for Sin, *we* should converse together as *Angels* do' (see *The Times Literary Supplement*, Dec. 27, 1991 and the second epigraph on p.xi of his book, *Style and Faith*).

[4] Given Hill's Platonic leanings, I am inclined to see here the influence of Porphyry's organisation of Plotinus's Neo-Platonic writings into a series of nine – the so-called *Enneads*. This type of scholastic intrigue is typical of Hill, and is similar to Joyce's intricate working methods in *Finnegans Wake*.

[5] The Anglo-Saxon poem 'The Dream of the Rood' is a possible model. What Hill is definitely opposing is that type of instrumental symbolism represented by Hart Crane's modern 'epic,' 'The Bridge,' or even Yeats' mechanical bird in 'Byzantium' – all 'Mechanics with a bit of string.' These images are too secular for him in their 'chain' of analogies, and far removed from what he calls 'The metaphysics of affinity.' See 'Improvisations for Hart Crane,' *Daedalus* (Fall, 2004), and 'On the Reality of the Symbol' in *Literary Imagination*, Spring 2004.

that intersects (Eliot's 'The point of intersection of the Timeless / With Time') with the 'cross' in the middle, when we descend into the realm of appearance away from reality, where all falls apart in a diverse number of broken rhymes. However, on occasion, the pattern ABBA itself is broken up, which suggests some kind of Miltonic confusion in Heaven, but also the possibility of a crossover (for good, one supposes) between the two realms, or spheres. Hill does little without forethought, and the scheme is metaphysical in its own right – away from the power of words themselves almost. There is a sense of language transcending into a type of 'meta-poetry' whereby the poet hopes to recover a genuine theological concept of the word as something more transcendent than mere Mallarméan conjuring. (Such 'emblems,' he insists in *Clavics*, in a Wittgensteinean way, 'Tell most without saying.') This careful craftsmanship makes *Oraclau* a highly-wrought volume, where, it might be said, style and faith meet. Hill's intention is to create a high pitch of intensity which avoids the spontaneity of what he terms 'the hag Sincerity.' In his essay on F.T. Prince he quotes the scholar approvingly to the effect that 'It is the artificiality of the word-order which makes possible the special beauties of both Della Casa and Milton. This alone makes possible the continuous interplay of the expected and the unexpected' – 'It is not the thoughts which make a Poet... but the locutions.'[6] Prose statements of this kind provide us with a clue to the artifice of *Oraclau* and *Clavics*.

As in earlier volumes, in *Oraclau* 'the dense and driven Passion' of Christ is celebrated, 'to Christ I look, on Christ I call' (the quotations are from the poetry of G. M. Hopkins).[7] For Hill, Christ is 'the satisfaction between the thieves,' 'a voice – / unchallengeable – of the foundations,' 'Supernature's light steadily prevails.' Christ's crown is 'A thorn-head spitting in a cage of fire' (possibly borrowed from Graham Sutherland's 'Thorn Head' paintings of 1945) – an image of the suffering of the martyrs down the ages – 'All saints on whose fierce faith the Church subsists.' In a blending of Romano-British worship of Mithras with that of Christianity, Jesus' life is seen as a 'Momentous instauration,' 'the sun / That's wedded to the Sphere.' This punning collocation we have encountered before in Hill's poem 'A Short History of British India (II)' (in *Tenebrae*) where we are told: 'The sun surmounts the dust.' Christ defeats time and history by breaking out of the

---

[6] 'Il Cortegiano: F.T. Prince's Poems (1938),' *PN Review* (September-October 2002).

[7] In his essay on Rhythm entitled 'Redeeming the Time' in *Agenda* (Autumn-Winter 1972-73) Hill argues that 'Hopkins's poetry established a dogged resistance. Both ethically and rhythmically, his vocation was to redeem the time.' ('Redeem the time' is a phrase repeated several times in Eliot's *Four Quartets*.)

tomb, defeating gravity, the 'weight of the world and the word,' overturning 'the great stone' of death.[8] He is the 'antichthon' (Hill's neologism is deliberately close to 'antiphon') – 'protean-fast' to earth's inevitable decay – Christ's 'gouged, / wrenched and sagging clay' as he has it in *The Triumph of Love* (thinking there specifically of Rouault's *Miserere*).[9] What is clear is that for the poet Christ overcomes 'the inert matter'[10] of the historical process. He is 'the stooped sun's blazon,' 'time's eclipse,' and the 'reach of resurrection.'

The term 'Clavics' appears first in *Oraclau* (in 'Music and faith consonant with our clavics') but the full implications of the word are revealed in the volume of that title, the fourth book of the projected series *The Daybooks*. Here the term is defined as 'the alchemy of keys,' suggestive of The Rock of St Peter, which ties in, one supposes, with the idea of that which is perdurable (the term may derive indirectly form Simone Weil's *La connaisance surnaturelle* where she defines 'clef' as 'la *technique transcendante*,' 'Harmonie, χγείς... proportion, union des contraires. Rythme... Equilibre'). *Clavics* is composed in a tight, elegiac structure reminiscent of the poem-sequences in *Tenebrae*, the poet exploring the power of the dramatic music of King Charles I's court composer, William Lawes, who was killed at The Battle of Chester in 1645.[11] The poem, in effect, is a celebration of his 'consort setts,' his 'textures of harmony,' of their 'sacramental belonging... with God's grammar.' The poet writes of 'infinite Clavics,' the 'paean' which transfigures our 'common pain.'

In *Clavics*, somewhere amid the (admittedly non-systematic) theology, lies the key (I use the word deliberately) to what Hill calls 'pitch.' Various critics have wrestled with the term in relation to Hill's work – to no avail it seems. Peter Robinson is not convinced by it as a theory, and neither is Christopher Ricks. The idea seems straightforward enough, if we are willing to accept Hill's personal, indeed eccentric, usage of the term. 'Pitch' is 'intrinsic value,' that place where the crafted details of a poem coalesce with deep belief. It is

---

[8] See Hill's essay 'Weight of the Word' in *Collected Critical Writings*, and Simone Weil's *Gravity and Grace* (1952) where she stresses the importance of imagination in creation: 'If the imagination is stopped from pouring itself out, we have a void poor in spirit... Imagination can fill the void.'

[9] The pun is on 'protein-fast,' and may suggest the desert father, St Simeon Stylites, starving on his pillar; but it also opposes Heraclitean change, the shifting metamorphic treacheries heard in 'Ovid in the Third Reich' for example.

[10] Hill quotes the phrase from a speech by Aneurin Bevan (himself named after a Welsh poet) talking of the miners' lot.

[11] Hill praises William Lawes as Pound praised his brother, Henry Lawes. Both were writers of masques, and Henry is mentioned in Hill's *Scenes from Comus*. (Lawes is Hill's musical hero as Purcell was Hopkins's.)

the poet's ability 'to sound out his own conceptual discursive intelligence... The poet is hearing words in depth and is therefore hearing, or sounding, history and morality in depth.'[12] It is viewed by him as a question of correct volition, moral rectitude, defeating what he calls the 'threads of chaos' – an achieved structure where energy and perception are at one, transfiguring a fractured world. 'The grace of music,' Hill writes, 'is its dissonance / Unresolved beneath resolution... Discord made dance.'

By contrast, 'tone,' in Hill's rather specialised application of the term, has to do with lesser (extrinsic) factors such as reception, esteem, status, and self-regard. It is that which 'draws attention to itself instead of to the object' (a phrase from his essay on the poetry of Keith Douglas, 1963), a 'false relation.' For Hill then it seems that poetry exists primarily to disturb and alienate, not to assuage and appease the reader. The poet stands or falls by the 'pitch' of his poetry alone, by the intensity of its achieved craft in relation to its spiritual matter. The distinction between 'pitch' and 'tone' then appears to be Hill's guiding principle when approaching any text in verse or prose. The problem is that the age, in all its supposed godlessness, is heedless of these matters, as Eliot observed in 'Ash-Wednesday': 'The air which is now thoroughly small and dry / Smaller and drier than the will...' For Hill, in rather blunter terms, Christ is 'A blessing trashed and in the bin.' 'We are in the midst of a spiritual confusion,' he says in one of his sermons, 'and that the worst confusion of all is the confusion regarding spiritual self-knowing' – 'Untenable still the timeless values' as he states it quite expressly in *Clavics*. Christ has been ousted by 'zane-sophistry's dead tyros' (a reference perhaps to Foucault and other Post-Modernists – Hill hates their 'Absolute relativity of mind' – and also possibly to the séances and 'automatic writing' of Mr and Mrs Yeats, and to Sylvia Plath and Ted Hughes' occasional resorting to the Ouija board.)[13] The church possesses nothing now but 'displaced gravity': it is a 'poor chantry-fane void of its king' (a phrase reminiscent of Shakespeare's 'bare ruin'd choirs'), a 'violent / disassembly' of creeds (particularly true, of course, of the present Anglican Communion), a 'gutted / tabernacle,' a 'time-struck Minster.'

All the mysteries are 'ravaged,' 'the grand paradigms' have gone. The preachers behave now 'as though the work of God hath come to nought' (quoting *Romans* v. 6), living in 'the shadows of the sacred groves,' – mere 'dealers in things despoiled' (one thinks of the 'Merovingian car-dealers' in *Mercian Hymns*). Faith now is like the mine's winding-gear, 'eaten by

---

[12] In his essay on Yeats, *Agenda*, Autumn-Winter, 1971-72.

[13] In his essay on C H Sisson, Hill writes of 'the Yeatsian-Jungian axis and its possible incitement of several forms of currently fashionable mysticism.'

rust / When not well-oiled' (the pun is obvious enough). Hill writes of 'the ephemeral / attacking the absolute,' of 'the secular conjuring of insurances,' 'the sacred name / of things betrayed,' 'Hag faith going the rounds,' 'the spirit in carnal disarray,' and 'the cherished stock / hacked into ransom and ruin.'[14] Hill's position is close to that of Eliot in 1931 when he wrote: 'The World is trying the experiment of attempting to form a civilised but non-Christian mentality. The experiment will fail; but we must be very patient awaiting its collapse; meanwhile redeeming the time; so that the Faith may be preserved alive through the dark ages before us; to renew and rebuild civilization, and save the world from suicide' (in 'Thoughts after Lambeth').

Both volumes evince a conviction that if organised religion has been marginalised in 'our disnatured century,' then so too has the poet. He no longer enjoys the privileges of the oracle composing sacred texts which engage the deepest resources of language – one aspect of the science of interpretation, or 'hermeneutics,' as analysed by Hans-Georg Gadamer in *Wahrheit und Methode* (1960). ('Hermeneutics' is a term the poet deploys several times in *Oraclau*.) Hill will have no truck with any of this mysticism, seeing the oracle's position as doomed. 'Poets are not legislators' he says, knocking Shelley on the head, 'unless they happen to be so employed, in government or law' (in his essay 'Our Word is Our Bond'). He is very pessimistic about the poet's position in modern society: 'the true poet is completely isolated,' he says. 'I am dubious… the whole business is dubious.' 'Poetry is eccentric / Labour of pride,' he believes, 'permitted to exist at the periphery of the Democratic machinery,' the poet 'a lame albatross' (echoing Baudelaire), 'the cracked fetish-monger.' 'Poetry has some of its teeth missing'; it is an 'Unfocused centre, stupefied at the margins.'[15] 'Most poetry today is fit for nothing but landfill' he asserted in his Inaugural Lecture as Oxford Professor of Poetry (30 November 2010), a 'scam' that fits in with 'the Education, the National Happiness, and The Bankers' Scams.' This is a very bleak outlook indeed, it must be said and also, I think, overly academic. Plenty of people read poetry today, but it is clearly not the sort of poetry Geoffrey Hill endorses. I think the canard he is attacking here is the undervaluing of poetry by the intellegentsia. This *trahison des clercs* has its roots in the type of thinking associated with Kierkegaard's argument in *Concluding Unscientific Postscript* (1843-46) that religious and ethical forms of life are centred in a stance of decisive action rather than in aesthetic contemplation ('the low

---

[14] See Eliot's 'The marred foundations we forgot, | Of sanctuary and choir' in *Four Quartets*. Hill's favourite Shakespeare poem is Sonnet 66: '…And purest faith unhappily forsworn…'

[15] On society's perceived condescension towards the poet, see the title of Hill's essay on Ivor Gurney – 'Gurney's "Hobby,"' (1984).

threshold of contemplation' as Hill calls it in *Clavics*). It is a perspective not shared by T. S. Eliot, for one, who writes, in *Four Quartets*, 'And any action is a step to the block,' a residue perhaps of the American's earlier Buddhist leanings. For Hill, in contrast, this type of determination is positive, indicating a commitment to a cause. The endorsement of this life of deeds is preferable to the anxious dithering of the cautious coward portrayed in 'Ovid in the Third Reich,' for example, in *King Log*. But equivocation, Hill infers, seems to constitute the whole of the poet's being: 'But we are commanded / To rise, when, in silence, / I would compose my voice' (the royal 'we' redolent of both political and ecclesiological patronage) in 'Men Are A Mockery Of Angels,' again in *King Log*. 'Should men stand by what they write?' Hill asks in *The Mystery of the Charity of Charles Péguy* – and his answer is, 'Well, yes, they should, and die for what they've written and believe in, rather than just stand by and watch.'

The deduction clearly is that there has been a loss of connection with Being, with the inner life of a subject or of a society, and the poet believes that only isolated remnants of a culture remain – traces, residues of 'intrinsic value' – what Ezra Pound calls 'the vestiges.' The position is close to Jacques Derrida's observation that as far as the majority is concerned 'there is no outside text' to live by today – the Frenchman sees this as a positive outcome; Hill does not – that there is little (outside the exception of scientific knowledge) that attracts conviction anymore. Hill would hope to counter this by 'rinsing' religious vocabulary of its secular taint. In this way sacral worth is restored through 'chrism' of the word, by the poet 'reaffirming the hierarchies,' rejuvenating 'the lost / amazing crown of faith,' as in section five of *Clavics*:

> *Making of mere brightness the air to tremble*
> So the sun's aurora in deep winter
> Spiders' bramble
> Blazing white floss
> Silent stentor! –
> Viscosity and dross
> No more amass
> At the centre
> *The whole anatomy of heaven and earth*
> Shewn as the alchemists declare it
> Poised beyond wrath
> Resurrection
> Of skin and bone
> To dispirit...
> The day cuts a chill swath,

> Dark hunkers down.
> I think we are past Epiphany now.
> Earth billows on, its everlasting
> Shadow in tow
> And we with it, fake shadows onward casting.

('Dispirit' carries that crucial Hillian complexity, suggesting a redemption of gloom, rather than an accession to it.) Hill's Christianity is more than just 'a richly available myth' — the phrase is Hill's own, summarising the poetic strategies of Sidney Keyes — and is best viewed as a sacramental 'symbolic grammar.' This grammar ('the syntax of becoming' as he calls it) takes us to the heart of his *poesis*. Grammar for Hill has its roots in existential crisis, and has affinities with Karl Barth's subjunctive articulation of the dilemma: 'as though we were able in some way or other to escape the *krisis* of God' the theologian writes.[16] This conditional voice informs and activates some of Hill's best work – 'Not as we are but as we must appear, / contractual ghosts of pity; not as we / Desire life but as they would have us live, / Set apart in timeless colloquy...' (in 'Funeral Music'); 'for the last rites of truth, whatever they are, / or the Last Judgement which is much the same, / or Mercy even, with her tears and fire, / he commends us to nothing...' (in *Péguy*). The tragic ambiguities are worked out in detail in Hill's intricate pointing, as in the line 'All things are, nothing is, to be saved' from *Oraclau* (remove the middle term and you have salvation, remove the first and you have nihilism – a conscious disposition first witnessed in the line '(There is nothing, over the white fields, amiss)' from an early uncollected poem called 'Summer Night,' which educes a similar concatenation of belief and unbelief). 'There is no grace of which all stand devoid' in section 139 of *Oraclau* embeds a similar equivocalness.

For Hill grammar is implicated in the fall of humanity, both in its simplest and in its most complex aspects. In this he is following Milton of *Paradise Lost* ('How art thou lost, how on a sudden lost, / Defac't, deflourd, and now to Death devote?') and of *De Doctrina Christiana* ('A diminution of the majority of the human countenance, and a conscious degradation of mind'). The argument, as Hill has it, is that the descent was a 'catastrophe' for 'inadequate, stricken humanity' – that our 'radically flawed nature' lost thereby our 'primal innocence among the groves,' suffering 'the taste of taint,' and the torments of the body's 'delicious sordor' (in *Oraclau*). Hill agrees with the Florentine Grammarians (especially Marsilio Ficino) that grammar is 'implicated in,

---

[16] Commentary on *The Epistle to The Romans*, sixth edition, OUP.

interpreting / the Fall,' and that our speech expresses 'our violent infirmities,' evincing 'the condemned stock / of original justice.' However, if as one we 'Fell in one root,' it was by Christ's blood that we were made free, 'recovered by one voice' in His redemptive act of self-sacrifice. The bloody myth of 'Genesis' becomes, in *Oraclau*, the mire of birth itself, the Fall summoned as the flesh-root of all corruption and pre-natal imperfection. We are informed of 'Despair attendant from the common cord,' 'the attendant bloodiness of birth,' the 'abysmal injury' wherein we came to breathe the 'lethal dust' of mortal life.[17] In the grammar of temporality, communion is wholly broken.

'We're not known to each other' the poet tells us, emphasising an inveterate solipsism (as he sees it) in the human condition. (He recognises the dangers of this position: in an interview with Bake Morrison, he tells us 'I think that if any poet says, "I write only for myself," he is also in great peril – he is in danger of solipsism and self-love.') This fractured condition results in a fragmented semantics, similar to the catastrophe which befell those who built The Tower of Babel. The result is mutual incomprehension and enmity. As Job phrases it: 'We cannot order our speech by reason of darkness.' Hill latterly may talk of 'this ever-doubtful certitude,' this 'strife of certitudes,' but perhaps the whole of his work, both in verse and prose, is best described as an agonising search for atonement and the abatement of original sin. Like Wordsworth in *The Prelude*, Hill believes in the affinity of 'spiritual love' with Imagination, and how 'Up to the height of feeling intellect' a 'dim and undetermined sense / Of unknown modes of being' can be deeply explored. The energy and intellectual conviction of his poetry make Hill stand out against the current of his time, and have nothing to do with the admiration of the contemporary crowd.

We await the other three volumes in the series with great interest. When the whole sequence is complete we may then appreciate in even greater depth the spiritual complexities partially explored in *Oraclau* and *Clavics*.

---

[17] The 'lethal dust' is also that of the coal mine, the miners who 'could ink your hymn sheets with black spittle,' and the murderous 'Seepage and sliding' of Aberfan. Hill's Blakean phrase for this condition is 'blood-intrigued Capital', with an intentional pun on London's indifference to 'child-victims in mill and mine.'

Josephine Balmer

A Day In The Life

Michael Longley: *A Hundred Doors* (Cape, 2011)
Brendan Kennelly: *The Essential Brendan Kennelly: Selected Poems*, edited by Terence Brown and Michael Longley (Bloodaxe Books, 2011)
Derek Mahon: *New Collected Poems* (The Gallery Press, 2011)

'A day here represents a life-time,' asserts Michael Longley of his beloved Mayo home in 'The Wren', a poem from his latest collection *A Hundred Doors*. Certainly for the last half-century or so it has seemed that we have lived that day – and its life-time – alongside a group of leading Irish poets which includes Derek Mahon, Brendan Kennelly and Longley himself, dedicating poems to each other, celebrating their mutual milestones, mourning the death of mutual friends. We feel we know every inch of Longley's Carrigskeewaun or Mahon's Kinsale or Kennelly's Dublin and Kerry. It seems, too, as if we have travelled with them through the course of their now long literary and personal lives as their poetry charts a progress from youthful promise to the rigours of old age. This impression is highlighted by a cross-referencing between the poets' work; for instance Mahon's early poem 'An Unborn Child' is dedicated to the young Michael and Edna Longley. Many years later, *A Hundred Doors* finds a much older Longley, now a grand-father several times over, contemplating an old photograph of his then-pregnant wife:

> Six months gone in your purple polo-neck
> And blue smock, and laughing, I remember,
> Because I have decorated with sea pinks
> Your black abundant hair...
> ('Foxgloves')

A Hundred Doors, Longley's ninth volume overall – and the fifth since he reignited his career with 1991's incandescent *Gorse Fires* – is an excellent place to start this day-in-a-life journey. As 'The Wren' exemplifies, its exquisite summoning of Longley's beloved Carrigskeewaun for his family's latest arrivals should continue to delight familiar readers, as well as draw in new:

>   ...bird's foot trefoil
> Among wild thyme, dawn and dusk muddled on the ground,
> The crescent moon fading above Mweelrea's shoulder
> As hares sip brackish water at the stepping stones...
>   ('The Wren')

There are shadows here too as old age's inevitable mourning for lost friends interrupts Longley's idyll: Dorothy Molloy, who had just published her first volume of poetry ('the poets you loved are your consorts now') or former childhood companions alongside the landlord of a favourite pub in which Longley had imagined his own perfect death and for whom, in memory, he now launches 'The toy lifeboat at my elbow with a penny' so that, in a moment, we are all transported back there with him. Longley's renowned and inspirational reimagining of ancient epic also makes a welcome return in 'Old Soldiers' and 'Cygnus', the latter an absorbing version of Ovid *Metamorphoses* 12.

But most importantly, there are new destinations here too, both geographical and poetic: the Shetlands, where Longley summons the ghost of Hugh MacDiarmid, the island of Paros, where he finds an echo of Greek poet Yannis Ritsos, or the New York Public Library in which he deciphers Edward Thomas's handwriting for Edna and recollects how the shell blast that killed Thomas 'still riffles the pages in the library'. The mention of Thomas ushers in a sequence of poems exploring Longley's own family members' experiences in the first World War, from an unknown namesake ('My wealden-distant cousin') chanced upon in a naval cemetery on Hoy to his father's citation for a Military Cross ('It is like a poem. It is better than a poem'). These short, pungent poems form the emotional heart of the collection and maintain, in fresh and rewarding new directions, Longley's continuing engagement with the still-reverberating past, to him the essential business of poetry:

> We need more angels, cloud-treaders, cherubic
> Instrumentalists, bomb-disposal experts.
> The sky is a minefield. We shall all get hurt.
>   ('Altarpiece')

These poems, in their turn, give way to a return to Longley's renowned and inspirational reimagining of ancient epic, which has so elegantly distinguished his volumes since *Gorse Fires*. In 'Old Soldiers', for instance, Longley characterises both his father and himself as the renowned veterans of ancient literature; Socrates 'stalking the battlefield at Delion' or Idomeneus at Troy, still just about able to throw and retrieve his spear, while the ghost of

Priam 'who loved his dogs/As my father his red setters and spaniels' recalls Longley's now iconic 1994 poem 'Cease Fire', the horrors of grief and old age still to come, when his former pet dogs will chew 'at his pathetic corpse's/ White head and white beard and bleeding genitals.'

Such work strikes to the heart of Longley's art – lyrical, moving, compassionate but above all connecting past and present, both distant and recent, in an urgent, common chain of humanity, looking unflinchingly into the abyss. Here he finds the perfect lyrical image or literary echo to enrich the readers, such as the 'white swan that flies above the bloody battlefield', as the metamorphosis of 'Cygnus' concludes. 'Would I add to the inventory?' asks Longley of his uncorrected *Collected Poems* in 'Proofs', tentatively answering himself with a typical list of found objects: 'A razor shell,/A mermaid's purse, some relic of this windless/Sea-roar-surrounded February quietude?' For this yet again almost perfect collection one might want for nothing more.

Longley appears again as joint editor, with academic Terence Brown, of Bloodaxe's new selected edition of Brendan Kennelly, *The Essential Brendan Kennelly*, a volume published to mark the poet's 75th birthday and including a welcome bonus CD of his own beautifully sonorous readings (his was apparently voted 'the most attractive voice in Ireland' in a radio poll). It opens with a selection of poems from Kennelly's earlier works including the mythic title poem of 1964's acclaimed *My Dark Fathers* and the nightmarish child's-eye views of 'The Kiss', 'The Smell' and 'The Horse's Head' alongside the typically visceral 'The Pig Killer' ('he raises a knife/begins to trace a line along the throat./Slowly the line turns red').

Things move up another gear with 1983's *Cromwell*, a world away from the rural childhood reminiscence which has often characterised recent Irish poetry and, even in the deft hands of poets such as Kennelly, can begin to appear well-trodden. In *Cromwell*'s vast mythic sequence, the country's arch-enemy appears in many guises, most traditionally as the chilling historical figure:

> Men die their different ways
> And girls eat cherries
> In the Christblessed fields of England.
> Some weep. Some have cause. Let weep who will.
> Whole floods of brine are at their beck and call.
> I have work to do in Ireland.
> ('Oliver to his Brother')

But he is also a modern-day companion, a daemon, a blooded conscience, for the poet's persona Buffún who has summoned him ('The butcher walked out of the door of my emptiness, straight into me.'), existing in a parallel present, demanding our attention and controversially, in places, our sympathy: 'I'm a friend of these ghosts,' as 'A Running Battle' concludes. 'They're mine'. Here Kennelly also begins to exercise ownership over more traditional English verse forms, in particular that of another, earlier Irish oppressor, Edmund Spencer, who himself appears in the sequence 'up to my bollox in sonnets'. As Longley and Brown note of Kennelly's art, the sequence operates in a 'perpetual now' in which Cromwell's evil is ever at our shoulder, underscoring not only its immortality but also its banality:

> ...I'm worn out from intrigue and work.
> I'd like a little estate down in Kerry,
> A spot of salmon-fishing, riding to hounds...
> Being a sporting chap, I'd really love to
> Get behind some of the best sides in the land.
> Manager, perhaps, of Drogheda United?
>   ('Manager, Perhaps')

Kennelly repeats this device, also to great effect, in 1991's influential *The Book of Judas* where, on the point of betraying Christ, his eponymous anti-hero has a vision of 'a bungalow two miles the Dublin side/Of Clonmel'('No Exit'.). Here Kennelly widens his canvas out from *Cromwell* as Judas's sin echoes throughout history and culture: 'Wars before and after/Howl through the last moments of my silver laughter', declares 'Last Moment'. The anthology also includes selections from 1995's *Poetry My Arse* as Kennelly turns his withering gaze on the world of contemporary Irish letters ('a map of that bashed old place/all the voices of the articulate dead') although, disappointingly, there is only one selection from 1998's superb *The Man Made of Rain* in which the poet squared up to a far more personal crisis, a triple heart by-pass.

Like Judas in 'I Never' – and so many of his own Irish poetic contemporaries – Kennelly also has ' a taste for Latin' and it is no surprise that he was drawn to the chaotic scabrous satire of Martial in which *Martial Art* (2003) finds not just the wit but the lyricism, handling the Latin poet's tricky changes of tone with characteristic bravura, underscoring with both precision and wit how 'Poems are drifters. A mind is an ocean'. So successful is Kennelly's engagement with the Latin poet that the latter's short lyrical forms later become infused with Kennelly's own work in his subsequent collection *Now* (2006), composed of pithy, three line poems. This is followed by 2009's *Reservoir Voices*, both represented in the volume by a rather inadequate single page, leaving the reader urgently required to search out more. Nevertheless the volume represents an admirable overview to this hugely gifted, original and influential poet. As Longley and Brown note in their Introduction, Kennelly's wide-ranging and ever-changing corpus can also lead to a 'varied' critical response but his poetic skill, its *sui generis*, is located precisely in the ease with which he can move between subject and especially tone – shifts that can confuse casual critics. As *Reservoir Voices*'s 'Poem' concludes: 'Words are wild creatures. Fly them home.' This excellent introduction should ensure a new generation of readers can do just that.

For Longley and Brown, the sheer volume of Kennelly's exceptional body of work could also 'pose a challenge to the bibliographer'. Derek Mahon's *New Collected Poems* might prove an equal problem for the textual critic as Mahon replaces the revisions of his earlier 1999 *Collected Poems* with a second definitive edition. This latest volume, published to celebrate Mahon's 70th birthday, now covers over fifty years of his poetry from 1968's *Night Crossing* to 2010's radiant *An Autumn Wind*, alongside a handful of new, uncollected poems. It opens with the youthful angst of 'Spring in Belfast', already exhibiting Mahon's deftness with traditional poetic forms, as well as his trademark displaced or disappointed romanticism as the young man resumes an already 'old conspiracy with the wet/Stone and the unwieldy images of the squinting heart'. It ends with the discursive 'Dreams of a Summer Night' in which the older Mahon listens to a Mozart concerto in Kinsale in mid-June. 'Can we relax now and get on with life?' he asks:

> Can we turn now to the important things
> like visible scents, how even silence sings?
> How we grew frolicsome one sunny June
> some sixty years ago at Cushendun
> in our young lives of clover, clock and cloud...
> ('Dreams of a Summer Night')

In between, all the early lyrics are here including the much-anthologised and still-compelling 'A Disused Shed in Co. Wexford' from 1975's *The Snow Party* and 'Courtyards in Delft', the eponymous poem from his 1981 collection, both, like all great poetry, continuing to offer up new secrets on each renewed reading. There are also the more expansive epistles of Mahon's middle period sojourns in New York and London before the renewed lyricism of his return to Ireland and Kinsale. Throughout, Mahon's irascibility at the distractions and inanities of the modern world - traffic noise, CNN, celebrity culture or 'the unreal world of cash and babble/ipod and car alarm' - is tempered, as ever, by his almost religious devotion to the belief that art in its widest sense is what will see us through, that 'poetry is the *real* mirage'. As he claims of Georges Braque's iconic images:

> Blurring the moon, they glide down tracts of time;
> abstracted from the facts and lost to sight,
> they save for us something of the creative dream.
> ('BIRDS')

Above all Mahon's poetry is that of allusion – and inclusion – not just through references to his fellow Irish poets such as Desmond O'Grady, Seamus Heaney or Paul Durcan alongside Longley, but also to the wider European canon, from Sappho, Ovid and Heraclitus to Camus, Malcolm Lowry or Montale, as well as the French poets Mahon has translated so successfully such as Gérard de Nerval or Phillipe Jaccottet. But there are also mentions of old black and white films, U2, Guns N' Roses and a perhaps surprising 'Ode to Björk', characterising the Icelandic singer as 'the dark swan of ice/and secrecy'. In particular Mahon is the supreme poet of ekphrasis, here the skill of reshaping the visual arts in to word, from Uccello's fifteenth century Gothic 'The Hunt by Night' through to the twentieth century abstractions of William Scott's 'Shapes and Shadows' or Howard Hodgkin's 'RAIN'. Throughout there is always the hope and humanity that has made him one of the ten most popular poets in Ireland as well as a worthy recipient of the prestigious David Cohen Prize. And so the volume concludes:

> I await the daylight we were born to love:
> birds at a window, boats on a rising wave,
> light dancing on dawn water, the lives we live.
> ('Dreams of a Summer Night')

As Mahon, Longley and Kennelly all move on into their eighth decades, their poetry – delicate, dissonant or discursive – seems always to move with us, whether for a day or, as has so often been the case, for a lifetime; to have become the lives we all live. 'There's no stranger,' Brendan Kennelly notes in 'Shaper' from his 2001 collection *Glimpses*, 'like the stranger/shaping the self'.

William Bedford

Exiles

David Harsent, *Night* (Faber, 2011)
Bernard O'Donoghue, *Farmers Cross* (Faber, 2011)
John Montague, *Speech Lessons* (Gallery, 2011)
Christine O'Neill, *The Scent Gallery* (Shoestring Press, 2011)
David Cooke, *In the Distance* (Night Publishing, 2011)

The heightened and the demotic are there from the very beginning of *Night*, 'out on the town' and 'up for Happy Hour', shuffling out of the prefatory poem to warn us 'There's a smell of scorch in the air. And the time to be gone has gone'. These are terrifying poems, nightmarish and difficult to understand, lurking at the edges of our minds like the visitations of the erotic Freud claimed to find in the unfulfilled wishes of dreams set at night. And the light is no safer, like something out of a horror film in 'The Hut in Question': 'Do you get what I mean if I speak of light – half-light – /that seems to swarm'. Harsent is *sui generis*, as poets of genius always are, and when we surrender to his vision, as Eliot told us to surrender to 'Lady, three white leopards sat under a juniper-tree', we will soon discover the exile that lies within each of us.

After the prefatory poem, 'Rota Fortunae' introduces the wheel of fortune, the capricious nature of fate, which is *Night's* philosophical universe. In its long-lined tercets, 'the turn of a key,/or else the turn of a card' might as easily 'turn you for home, or take you to the brink'. In the poem 'Ghosts' which follows, the dead 'shuffle up as if they stood on the edge/of night so a nudge would tip them over', and then we are in to a sequence of 'garden' poems. But these are not gardens of paradise or Marvell's places of solitude. As 'The Garden in Fading Light' tells us: 'Here is your key. It was specially cut. If the door/to the garden blows shut as you enter, at least/you'll have your own key, though the way out is not // really the same'. The place hardly seems to be a garden at all with 'the litter, the rat-run under the floor,//the bat in the rafters', but then visitors to gardens 'forget that night/falls more readily in gardens' with its 'note of panic evening brings to birdsong.' In the rest of the sequence, 'the night's blood-hunt' has a woman in her twilight kitchen caught in 'that moment from the myth/in which you look back and everything goes to hell'; a sunlit garden where 'you're on a wish//and a promise, adrift in white's slow creep/away and over the edge'; a dream garden where a couple could be sharing 'love in a mist' or equally the 'Stockholm syndrome'; and finally a garden goddess who is 'as likely to spit in your eye as lay/a calming hand on your cheek'. These are gardens always on the edge of rain, and the goddess looks 'as if she had once been the victim/of a random attack'.

Harsent's lurid, flickering landscapes are as blighted as the fragments of Eliot's *Sweeney Agonistes* or David Lynch's unnerving films, an urban nightmare finding no safety in town or country. In 'Scene One: A Beach' the protagonist finds himself 'pitched up on some shoreline/like any piece of wreckage' where 'Everything I once recognised as mine/is strange to me now'. In the visceral 'Spatchcock', lovemaking is parodied with the narrator 'slipping up from behind to cop a feel' and spatchcocking the woman. 'The Queen Bee Canticles' has a priest 'who preached only sin and redemption' becoming 'from neck to scalp/a spinning ball of bees', so thrilling the hive queen that 'she stung/his lips, his tongue, his eardrums, his eyelids, his eyeballs'. These are hard imaginings to endure. And the tortures inevitably lead to disturbances of the mind, brilliantly realised in the volume's title poem, 'Night', with its bleak evocation of how 'it feels when the mad machine cranks up/and the room breeds shadows out of dusk'. In such poems, we are taken on a redemptive journey through anguish and pain, culminating triumphantly with the noirish quest-poem 'Elsewhere.'

The septets of 'Elsewhere' pulse with the rhythms and repetitions, the verbal play and chiming alliteration of Muldoon's 'Incantata'. But if Harsent is being playful, it is definitely a dangerous game. His Orpheus wanders the back-streets of his own mind, 'a figure frozen/by guilt' in search of the woman he abandoned. Reliving the past in a futile quest, his only companions his memories and a feral dog. Harsent's Orpheus is an exile who cannot be at home anywhere, journeying through a constant dream of elsewhere. It is a surreal 'elsewhere': the garrulous barman and nightclub hostess, the shop window mannequin stepping down to the pavement, the fortune teller and the 'sad old sack' living rough on a beach – all seem to know more of Orpheus's life than he does himself, and bring nothing for consolation. And after everything he has experienced, 'a sudden wash/of music, *lachrimae*' from the past 'is all it takes' to set him out on the road once again. That such bleak encounters with the night bring a deep feeling of hope is a magnificent achievement.

Titles can be a writer's gift to his readers, the absence of the possessive in *Farmers Cross* and *Finnegans Wake* offering and withdrawing their obvious religious meanings, and leaving us with the task of discovering where we are: 'cross' about what? 'wake' to what? There is more going on in *Farmers Cross* than O'Donoghue's deceptively genial tone might suggest, and the epigraph from Basho gives us another clue, as epigraphs should: 'Of all the many places mentioned in poetry,/the exact location of most is not known for certain'. O'Donoghue's poetry has always been rooted in his Cork childhood, which is precisely why it has such deeper resonances, a point Henry James would have immediately understood.

Forms of exile recur in O'Donoghue's work, but the opening poem, 'Bona-Fide Travellers'. shows us that you can be an exile in your own country. An ancient law of Ireland 'meant you had to be from somewhere else/to get a drink' out of the usual drinking hours. That 'was all right with us', the insider casually remarks, but then:

> The trouble came when, dozing
> on the boat, you half-came round and saw
> the seabirds bathing, the gannet plunging
> towards his bath, and battalions
> of unknown children, speaking in accents
> different from their parents.
> ('Bona-Fide Travellers')

This sudden blaze of poetry is a familiar feature of O'Donoghue's *ostranenie*, his 'making strange', and takes us straight to the heart of the poem: 'In the real world, of course, there's no such person/as a Bona-Fida traveller'.

Such geographical displacements are immediately followed by the perspectives of 'History.' In what sounds like a family anecdote, the poet tells us of a child 'aged four in 1865' being 'lifted on to her father's shoulders/at Abraham Lincoln's funeral', an experience the father tells the child never to forget. She passes the memory on, and it rings down the generations until the poet himself becomes the latest guardian of the past:

> so what I say to you is: never forget
> that you once read something by someone
> who said they had known when they were young
> someone who said their father told them
> they had been to Abraham Lincoln's funeral.
> ('History')

Here, despite the prosaic language and the colloquial ease of the metre, a glimpse of what history actually means leaps off the page. The notion of Joycean epiphanies sounds far too grand for such quiet moments, but that is what repeatedly gives O'Donoghue's work its distinctive quality of illumination.

The translation of 'The Wanderer' darkens the theme of exile. This was a risky venture into harsher metres and imagery than O'Donoghue usually enjoys, but the experience of translating *Sir Gawain and the Green Knight* seems to inform his rendering of the Old English. This elegiac wanderer listens to the radio in a world where the 'bombs have won out' in 'a desert of tar' where 'once there were streets.' The catastrophes tell us what we already know: he is a 'refugee' rather than the 'wanderer' of the title.

Farmers Cross is full of such wanderers and refugees. In 'Rubbish Theory' 'the man who planted our mountain ash' is now 'buried himself in New South Wales'; in 'Crumpsall', a girl who emigrated to work in Manchester is 'woken by the noise/of boots on cobbles', and wonders 'when could she go home, and lie in her own bed/thinking back to work-sirens and trains'; 'Gunnar too would have fled Iceland' in 'Freyfaxi'; '"I suppose we'll see them here no more"' Jer Mac says in 'Tea Dolls' of the poet and his two sisters as they depart for England. More hopefully, 'Emigration' tells us 'Unhappy the man that keeps to the home place' and never has the chance to 'tell the world's wonders,/before settling down by his hearth once again'. But the 'world's wonders' include Dachau in 'In Bavaria,' and memories of Verdun in 'Mere Planter and Fior-Ghael,' casting a chilling shadow over celebrations of 'revered British virtues'. Even the title is a reminder of forms of historical exile. These poems of exile remind us we are only here as travellers. Even at home, the journey must end, an end beautifully captured in the volume's final poem, 'The Year's Midnight': 'it was as predictable as the seasons/that you would die on the shortest day,/a day when the world was least enlightened/ and the shades fell not long after 3 p.m'. As always, O'Donoghue's cadences are beguiling. His vision offers quiet consolation.

John Montague is celebrated for his 'insistence on mischief' and the gift is there in 'One Bright Sunday' with its recognition 'that grown-ups of some importance/may still frolic like infants', and the riskiness of 'I saw a tiny Christ/caper on the cross // silent as a salamander/writhing in fire' in 'Baldung's Vision', but the heart of *Speech Lessons* for me lies in the poems dealing with Montague's childhood.

Born in Brooklyn, he returned to Ireland in a kind of reverse-exile, to hear 'the rats scamper // in the shadowy rafters over my head'. There is a new nostalgia here for a world of carts and horses, but Montague is too intelligently sceptical not to recognise 'the future, already whirling past' the 'long hangar of the turf shed.' As a 'bare-legged boy', he was told by his grandfather to *'Take time to thrive, my ray of hope'* until *'your wings/are feathered fit to soar'*, and for decades he has triumphantly done that.

'Bibles massive as flagstones' feed the imagery of these poems, as his grandfather's clock inspires the metre 'until he stopped short,/never to go again/in Garvaghey graveyard'. But though the poems here are ostensibly for Montague's grandfather, as so frequently in Montague's work he is drawn back to the women who people his imagination. Remembering 'the grave dug open/to admit another daughter' and his grandfather's '"large families were common then"', the poet wants to know 'what would your poor wife have to say?' He has 'only one photograph' of this 'tightly corseted woman' who finally 'died, in childbirth', and yearns to save her from the 'patriarchal night' which enslaved her generation.

That is not how the woman herself sees things: '"I was a flesh-and-blood woman,/the strongest of my house,/so do not distil me into dream!"' she insists, leading the poet to recall 'a rare flash of anger' of one of his aunts, condemning the feckless men drinking whiskey '"while/we hungry children cried"'. There are rural pieties in these memories, but also tougher, harsher voices resenting the poet's own patriarchal interpretations of their lives:

> *"And who are you, anyway, you whippersnapper,*
> *sharing our family secrets with the world:*
> *so I say again, have a titter of wit, man!"*
>   ('In My Grandfather's Mansion')

There is a colloquial energy and earthy realism in these poems. We see a boy carrying 'bristling bundles of straw/from the haggard or/barn to the byre' and collecting roadside flowers for an aunt who brushes them aside, his disappointment softened by time as he realises the 'bigger disappointment/for her, no longer/a dancing girl/given bouquets/by gallant men/but only wildflowers/by a little boy'; and movingly again, 'as my bone-tired aunt/bends to her evening task' the poet asking 'Is that a child asleep/in the crib of straw,/or a trick of the light?' A remote way of life is resurrected in these fine poems, exuberant with the wisdom of lived experience.

In a quiet way, Christine McNeill keeps form courteously in the background until the content forces you to realise just how delicate her touch has been. She has translated Rilke's *The Life of the Virgin Mary* and *The Book of Hours*, and studied Jungian psychology. Anne Beresford and Pauline Stainer come to mind when reading her visionary and sometimes quite shocking poems.

The ghosts of Rilke and Jung haunt *The Scent Gallery*. Early mankind 'wanting to reach/the God behind rock' 'blew the hand's imprint/onto the stone,' and McNeill sees her own quest as poet in similar terms:

> If I were to do it in words,
> would you receive
> the sounds of my soul,
> answer *I'm here*
> and *You need to go it alone?*
>   ('An act of prayer')

In 'Guide book' a child imagines the ringing of church bells 'as if pulling down God'; 'Diviner' reveals its searcher discovering a medieval village 'buzzing with people'; a 'Vietnamese sponsored child' in the title poem writes 'that he could smell *love* in a green field'. Epiphanies shine throughout *The Scent Gallery*. In 'House', the house of cards of childhood becomes a real dwelling in Norfolk, vulnerable to coastal erosion on 'the edge of the cliff', an image of our greater vulnerability to time. 'Confirmation' tells the stories of three generations of women, linked by acts of human kindness and the scent of rose petals emanating mysteriously from favourite pieces of porcelain.

'Confirmation' plays with the religious idea of communion, 'tasting for the first time the sacred', but the presence of the 'Vietnamese sponsored child' hints at the wider, darker world that is the concern of these poems. 'Unearthly hour' has a suicidal young woman saved by the kindness of a passing stranger with the simple words '*Is something wrong?*' The awful past tense of 'Release' shows the brutalised victim of an arranged marriage experiencing a glimpse of freedom as she reached for a plant and 'cupped it in both hands and cried'. Survivors of Auschwitz and Bosnia, the savage butcheries of war and crime and rape, talk from the shadows of these poems, unflinching encounters of the best with the worst. This is a world where we are all, in one sense of another, refugees.

But the best of us is often seen in the way we care for the old, beautifully, earthily, comically explored in 'Moving train', 'Martha's reverie', 'Friday 3 p.m.', 'Praying in secret' and 'Eclipsed moon'. '"*Now you look lovely!*"' someone says in 'Martha's reverie', saying it all. And the 'all' of Christine McNeill's vision is brought together in her homage to Carmen Herrera, 'I became a famous artist in old age'. 'My joints ache/with old age' the artist tells us, 'but when I begin to paint // I'm like a tree/that spring touches with green'. '*You need to go it alone*' is not the message I find in *The Scent Gallery*.

David Cooke found his voice early. His first volume, *Breughel's Dancers*, was published in 1984, but some of the poems in that collection had already received a Gregory Award. *In the Distance* collects those early poems together, adding a substantial selection of exciting new work. The poem 'Bruegel' announces his obsessions from the start. 'There are times your dancers annihilate/the humanist in me', he tells us, the reasons graphically clear, the rhyme anticipating a lifetime's struggle with language:

> Blind sticks jerk
> as they stumble on the bank of a stream;
> while we tread the limits of what words mean.
>
> ('Bruegel')

Even in poems of childhood such as 'Down', Cooke is already a poet with his 'ear to the ground', sensing 'far off/a thunder of horses trapped'; imagining in 'Hill-Fort' 'dogs/and people, their utensils // ranged around fire'. The child becomes the man in 'Visiting', still following his grandfather in his imagination, 'running so breathlessly/beside you as you stride/onwards, the castle of yourself,/across rough fields // of thistle and clover'. In 'A House in Mayo,' the wisdom earned is salutary, the tracks other people left behind smothered; 'all I ever found were mine'.

Early poems such as 'Epilogue' were already looking beyond a childhood of 'snug interiors/where Christ's heart glowed' to the politics implicit in *The Foggy Dew* and the culture which came with Virgil and Catullus. In the new poems, the adult questioning of 'The Catechism', with its claim 'Just goodness wasn't enough/when even Socrates wasn't a saint', comes as no surprise. In 'Luther', the memory may be of school where the reformer was thought to be 'damned', but the poet now recognises in Luther's 'self-contempt' the 'knowledge that leads/to a choice that is existential'. Politics here are realistic, not sectarian, the poet's father in 'My Father, the Pragmatist', having no theory beyond *'that the whole world/looks out for its own'*. The best wisdom is a mature sense of reality, and 'Gambler' achieves this with brilliant wit and humanity. The poet's father may never have read Pascal, but he knew 'what he needed to know/about risk', and made sure he 'went to Mass on Sundays', because 'The odds on heaven were evens'.

Memories of a West of Ireland childhood haunt these poems, but Cooke is not treading ground already made familiar by others. Growing up in England, his 'making strange' grows naturally out of his exile between two countries. The limewashed pieties of rural Ireland are here, but in a wider context of European culture and history. Calvin and John Coltrane rub shoulders, in Cooke's imagination, with Arnaut Daniel and the musicians of 'Chicago's South Side.' 'So I start again from a dark wood' he tells us in 'In the Middle of the Way', but it is a dark wood he is stringently illuminating. After a long silence, David Cooke has burst back into life, in a welcome and gifted performance.

Belinda Cooke

Snicking at Edges

Gill McEvoy: *The Plucking Shed* (Cinnamon Press, 2010)
Jean O'Brien: *Lovely Legs* (Salmon Poetry, 2009)
Louise C. Callaghan: *In the Ninth House* (Salmon Poetry, 2010)
Matthew Barton: *Vessel* (The Brodie Poets, 2010)
Tony Roberts: *Outsiders* (Shoestring Press, 2010

Gill McEvoy in *The Plucking Shed* gains her inspiration from difficult life experiences – the early loss of her mother, and husband, father's subsequent death and her own cancer. The resulting poems are tough, harrowing, and tightly crafted. She is a poet who doesn't take any prisoners.

Her reaction to visitors' platitudes during her own illness: 'I am diamond, carborundum, / and I wipe out fools' ('Message to the Well-Meaning') reflects this toughness. The roots of this are suggested in 'My Mother's Kitchen' where, fearing the father's return, the mother 'squares herself to face the door' while the child starts to 'grab the table'. Later, however, in the poem 'Scissors', the scissors act as a family mascot of shared uncompromising characteristics with the father now a less threatening yet small-minded individual to whom she conveys unconditional familial love. Here we have a bearing things out 'to the edge of doom':

> That absence of you, for example, my father,
> whose telephone number I still have by heart,
> can still count on my fingers the things you kept
> in your kitchen drawer: a knife, a fork,
> one tablespoon, three teaspoons – the scissors,
>
> that real word that had you, after my mother's death,
> snicking at edges, severing frills,
> shearing your life to so little.
>
> ('Scissors')

It is in the poems dedicated to her husband, however, that she is at her most harrowing. Here I defy anyone not to be moved:

Last night cloud came down like a weight
of feathers, whited out our little house.

I wheel you out to say good morning to the day.
You waggle useless hands as if to part the mist

that curtains you from me. Soft as heartbeats I can hear
the steady weep of wet from vanished trees.

The world is locked away; no insects, birds.
Their absence haunts the day.

Our breath hangs on the milky air,
like words we'll never say.

I push the body-shell from which the *you* has gone –
ask myself, how long can this go on?
('Locked Away')

The dominance of monosyllables and full or close to full rhymes, particularly the concluding couplet, establishes a clarity of tone to support the absolute honesty of her emotions. She skilfully merges the literal description of her husband's ineffectual hand movements with imagery of separation to show both his deterioration and the way she has been cut off from him and also that ongoing life that is at present 'locked away'. In the face of all this emotion the poem does not shy away from her both wanting and dreading the end at the same time as it conveys a deadly calm stasis to reinforce the way her life has been put on hold.

After more searing poems on the illness and loss – describing how his absence 'Made me touch the edges of your missing,/ cut my fingers on its jagged glass' ('Edges') – she brings Finbar the man back to life for her reader. Note, here, how the apples' image balances the two stanzas to connect Finbar's qualities with the totality of her loss:

The stars here are like apples
crowding the tree.
You could have picked them one by one,
kept them in the pocket
closest to your heart.

> But it is I who watch the stars,
> I, who cannot name them as you did.
> The pockets of my heart are filled
> with holes, not stars, the bright apples
> always out of reach.
> ('For Finbar')

Then, like Indiana Jones, no sooner are we out of the snake-pit than we are forced to confront a line of hostile natives as she deals with her own illness: 'No-one speaks. My tongue is nailed down./ Words have swum away' ('Diagnosis'). However, we are also given Macbeth's drunk porter scene for light relief as she rounds off the collection with a *carpe diem* exuberance. Here, having cheated death, she relishes the small pleasures of the natural world. Throughout, whatever the emotion, she keeps her eye closely focused on the craft of the poem – there is not a superfluous word to be found.

*

Jean O'Brien's *Lovely Legs* immediately entices with its eye-catching cover, catchy title and her clever and complex opening poem, 'Masks'. Here, sustaining a sinister tone throughout, she interweaves fear, regret, sexual tension and power relations established via the shocking image of a man whose face is covered with bees, later juxtaposed with a woman's dying wish. The poem is intriguingly ambiguous as to who has the power, the man or the bees. He starts out with 'the queen snared in a cage under his chin' yet by the end of the poem it is he who 'moves gingerly'. Strong active verbs reinforce the idea of an inexorable, frightening encounter. The poem leaves us feeling that life is dangerous, yet vibrant, the natural world and human relations a realm of strong colour rather than pastel shades – of intense sensations that are ours for the taking, shown particularly here in its concluding stanza:

> Elsewhere, a woman wants sunflowers
> on her grave. She loves
> their pomp and majesty; wants them
> to face her and not the sun,
> wants their seeds to fall into the earth,
> mingling with her marrow and take root.

There are a number of poems of this quality in the collection. She is at her best when she draws on the natural world to meditate on human issues.

Consider the following poem, for example, where she cleverly uses the laburnum as an extended metaphor to explore the nature of truth and lies:

> The bright light togs itself out
> in the yellow racemes of laburnum –
> a lemon surprise to trap birds and flies,
> it spreads its poison gift-wrapped.
>
> Truth is a labyrinth, obscured
> like the laburnum that lies between
> the sapwood and the heartwood
> we sense it just below the surface.
> The hard outer bark, a polished lustre,
> something lacquered over.
> ('Fighting Talk')

Here we see how much she gets beneath the surface of the image in order to make it really do its work in exploring its analogies with the poem's subject matter. She thus enables the laburnum to act as a powerful extended metaphor for the nature of truth and lies and how that impacts on human relationships.

She also includes a number of strong family poems. We have the harrowing poem where her father has to break the news to her and her sister of their mother's death: 'our lives a fulcrum till he spoke / then the dreadful balance tilted' ('When Childhood Broke') as well as poems that include some lovely images of her mother as a young woman: '… She is shattering the light/ of the sun, I hold her image framed' ('The Arc of a Swing in Autumn'). She also includes a particularly touching and visually exact description of her child:

> For now she sits with her sea anemone fingers
> wrapped around a pencil that she mows
> across the white page like someone
> cutting a lawn in regular sweeps.
> She is writing her own story
> moving herself into the centre of her life,
> not loaned, or copied, borrowed, just hers.
> ('Time Traveller')

The determined movements of the child's little fingers across the page are strongly visualized to represent her right to individuality. The image is all the more poignant following on from the poem's earlier establishment of infant vulnerability and our shared destiny of death: 'Her golden head a skull then, bone white, / small enough to fit snug in a hand'.

The only weakness in this otherwise fine collection is the occasional tendency to overwrite and explain away some of the poems. This is where a final edit might have made a difference. By way of example consider the following poem 'Crossing' where she wonders at what point the spirit passes from the body – that moment of crossing over. She begins:

> You lay rigid
> like the stone effigy
> of Eleanor of Aquitaine,
> hands holding a prayer book
> across your breast
> just the same.
> Behind you at the window
> wind threw a squall of rain
> ('Crossing')

A good start appropriate to the subject matter, the effigy image, though not unusual, nevertheless creating the right tone of sepulchral calm and the reader can be there with her as a watcher over the dead. Then however she spoils this shared experience by, in the next line, explaining the poem away:

> like memory,
> as if all your possibilities
> were alive and well
> and not as is,
> dead and done.

This need for a little more honing is not great enough to mar the overall collection but based on the theory that less is more it might have enabled the many quality poems in this fine collection a better chance to shine.

*

Louise C. Callaghan's *In the Ninth House* will provide an immediate shock of recognition for those of us with our own stories of poverty or those inherited from our parents. She achieves this in some of the opening poems via the concrete detail of carefully selected details: 'to see their baby among stockingless legs / and broken-down shoes – her bare bottom'. ('Two-and-a-Half') or in the painful accounts of her very uncertain self struggling to read, an experience metonymically conveyed via the drawer used for her reading materials: '…still feel that dry disagreeable pull / of a drawer without runners'. ('Reading and Writing'). The trauma of that early failure is even more poignantly conveyed in another poem:

> The trick is not to let anyone
>
> see the wet-stain on the back
> of your school skirt.
> You remain on in the squat chair,
> but really you disappear.
> ('The Trick Is…')

However, vivid, immediate and poignant as many of these uncertain inroads into life are shown to be, there is more to this collection than simply childhood memories. Such selective sharp images all contribute to a more complex scheme suggested in the collection's title. The cosmological term the 'Ninth House' signifies the mind's symbol-making capacity. Callaghan's poems, for the most part, consist of fairly minimalist images that build to a cohesive whole in an architectonic form of free association. Throughout this process she maintains a consistency of voice: that same, uncertain child who struggled to read, or climb trees with her sisters is similarly uncertain in her adult encounters, such as when she says of Sappho: 'What troubled her/ now troubles me' ('Fragments'). This free association combined with a fragile voice continues with further classical connections. She begins with the fairly overt linking of her parents' courtship and Athena in 'Athena in Mourning' and then continues in the poem that immediately follows it to paint the connections with a lighter brush:

> It seems to me
> > three decades later
> > and more
>
> the sad arc of her helmet
> > is bowed for
> > some mortal loss:
> …

>   how perfectly
>   they matched.
>   I can hear them laugh.
>
>   But too easily she snapped.
>   In pity and sorrow,
>   Athena took her name.

There is a lovely economy and restraint to these lines achieved through the simplicity of the images and the plain statement of stark emotions, a restraint found in many of her poems, whether they are aiming to suggest a more complex interaction with the natural world, such as this description of picking potatoes:

>   like dappled stars,
>   luminous planets revolving in the
>
>   Ninth House of ones's natal chart.
>   Bunched in a dish they smell of clay.
>   ('Homeguard Earlies')

Or this more haiku-like crystalline observed moment:

>   A harebell, blue as the sea,
>   in a bitter wind, anchored deep,
>   like the Muire-blue shining out
>   from Harry Clarke's chapel window.
>   ('Winter in Inis Meáin')

For the most part this collection works by providing such images and leaving the reader to make the connections but occasionally we have Callaghan wanting to tell as well as show. When she does have something she wants to state she does it with a similar sense of economy combined with that same touching vulnerability that has sustained the collection throughout:

>   I wanted to say something that
>   wouldn't wash away the next day,
>   catch the music of the waves –

spray clawing the air as it fell back.
I have watched, listened with Winter,
bitten into silence. Said what I can.
</br>   ('Immram: Inis Meáin)

*

Matthew Barton's collection *Vessel,* offers us poetry of real class. It is not surprising to discover that he is the winner of many prestigious poetry awards including second prize in The National Poetry Competition. His ability to select the apposite phrase or word, the richness of his diction, his subtle observations on relationships and the natural world result in highly individual poems edging into a spiritual/philosophical view of how objects and beings inhabit the world or, indeed, how the world inhabits them. Combining craft and intellect he offers the reader a fresh view of how things connect. This he manages to sustain in poem after poem. Consider, for example, his view of nettles:

> I've always liked them – not just for the sharp
> respect they inspire, but because they seem
> galvanized in the defence of some
> frail underside of innocence.
> </br>   ('Nettles')

You feel as though the nettles in his poem have souls and yet a closer look shows how the poem works via a careful build-up of vivid, tough descriptions of the nettles: 'electric', 'tense', 'leathery green', 'bristling ring', 'live wires', 'pungent', 'fury of belief', 'sparking static' all working towards the dramatic contrast of that concluding phrase of vulnerability: 'frail underside of innocence'. Here is a man who knows how to use his adjectives (and we all thought that wasn't allowed). The effect is rich, sensuous language that transforms the nettles into something transcendental at the same time as it leaves you thinking: ah yes, that is what I've always felt about nettles but never quite had the words to say. It is this kind of skill that gives a dazzling quality to many of his poems.

In 'Buzzard' there is a complex interplay between the actor and the acted upon. Is it the buzzard or the earth that moves? Note also the use of religious words that contributes a grandeur to the poem – a feature common to many of his poems:

The buzzard is absolute –
ly still: the world revolves.

Now and then the ground
kneels in to him: its prayer
is full of flesh which he exalts
to weightlessness.

A poem that really stands out in this collection is 'Utter' with its interplay of notions of the river (as generic) and Ophelia. Again we wonder who is the actor and whom the acted upon:

> In pools
> she slips to stillness and her mind
> widens to conceive the cold
>
> imprint of heaven; now starts to gather
> lazy momentum, twists a shining
> umbilicus from emptiness. Then shatters
>
> to splinters that heal under, pour
> out whole again. The river winds
> me around her finger, mutters
>
> nothings, insinuates her chaste
> tongue into my ear. Keeps going deeper
> into herself, giving herself
>
> utterly to what utters her.

The poem's momentum is achieved through the well-chosen use of enjambement to convey the river's movement, combined by the build-up of active movement verbs – 'slips', 'widens', 'twists', 'shatters', 'winds', 'insinuates'. One feels Barton has relied on a combination of close observation and Wordsworthian style 'recollected in tranquility' which includes a memory at least of Millais's painting though fortunately not enough to reduce this to an ekphrastic poem. The poem takes us in all sorts of directions: with the repackaging of the stock phrase – 'the river winds / me around her finger', we journey into the poet's mind yet the poem is also a tribute to Shakespeare and the iconic status his Ophelia has acquired in our culture, one that far outweighs her role in the play.

In this collection Barton also includes a number of personal poems and does not steer clear of expressing the tensions within relationships but with the same nuanced eye as we have seen in the above poems. This is a collection that will leave you wanting to seek everything he has written (his first collection is *Learning to Row*, Peterloo Poets, 1999) because of the sheer quality of what is here.

*

Outsiders is Tony Roberts' third collection. As with his earlier books, he combines the personal with poems on art and history. He opens with a quotation from Herzen which clearly sets out what he sees as the importance of culture and human relations to our happiness: 'Art and the summer lightning of individual happiness: these are the only real goods we have'. The best poems in this collection certainly convince us of this, interweaving his cultural experience and human relationships in a moving way.

The Outsiders is a substantial collection. It divides into three sections, the last focused on the jazz clubs of New York and Paris of the late 1950s. The other two sections draw a great deal on his own travel, particularly in Scandinavia and Russia and the second of these sections, 'Outsiders', places particular emphasis on the experience of exile. The poems will be particularly appealing to those with a specific interest in European culture, not to mention fifties' jazz. He also includes a number of powerful poems on classical music.

A poem which is particularly successful in merging emotion and culture is the one based on Jutland. Here, he focuses on the survivor whose relationship has been thwarted by the man's death: '…Nana,/ lost in her eighties and turned out / like a doll for family affairs'. He then provides a clever interplay between her 'understanding' with her intended versus his understanding before death:

> And what was his understanding,
> this young seaman on *The Black Prince,*
> far astern of the British fleet off Jutland,
> steaming through darkness for the line of ships
> midnight would show to the enemy?
> ('Lost')

One of the most impressive poems in the whole collection is one where the entire focus is on emotion. Consider the following powerful lines dealing with tensions in a relationship with the protagonists on a day out together. This is powerful stuff:

> Supposedly they are out to air the bruising.
> They avoid the fell, skirt patches here
> where Rydal Water threatens tussock grass.
> They're slowed as much by torment as by afternoon.
> She asks him where they're going now
> and knocks aside the hand that lifts the map.
>
> Cheap pun, and yet he cannot bring himself to care –
> another infidelity. And then, returning past the gates,
> she stoops to pick the showiest leaf.
> It is something to remind her of her misery.
> If the worst comes to the worst, there is acceptance.
> After all, there are so many fallen leaves.
> ('The Gates at Crow How')

Though there are phrases that might be cut to allow the reader a little more intelligence: 'They're slowed as much by torment as by afternoon', 'cheap pun', 'it is something to remind her of her misery', the moment of irritation combined with the poignancy of the unhappy relationship really impacts and leaves one feeling that one would like more poems with this kind of emphasis.

Roberts can also be very funny. Take, for example, the catchy titled poem: 'When I think of all the women who have drunk my wine' which does essentially what the title suggests providing us with a list of such women, and in the process a very recognizable experience of drinking sessions with people from one's past. He amusingly concludes:

> And Rachel in Paris,
> shaking her pale, apologetic face
> over the last of the Muscadet,
> which you sent me back to reclaim
>
> the hoover racing at her side.

In his music poems he is good at interweaving ideas of music and sexual desire: 'She recalled his nervous hands framing her own / his kindness stirred to those twelve horn calls' ('Elmira'), or he rather amusingly plays on the musical term of the title '*Con abbandono*' where he describes the instruments:

>   ...making off

across the lawns of the Esterházy palace,
one at a swallow-tailed time:
the wanton oboes and the horns,
engorged bassoons, priapic strings,
the carnal bass drum *con abbandono*.

Taking the collection as a whole, his wide-ranging interests have a lot to offer the reader, though occasionally, where erudition supersedes emotion, he risks excluding his reader and might keep this in mind when making choices for inclusion. As with O'Brien again it is a case that less might be more. Ultimately emotion-driven lyrics are always going to allow for the most universal appeal.

NOTES FOR BROADSHEET POETS

Agenda Poetry Competition: comments by Patricia McCarthy

Results

First Prize: £1,000
   Kim Lasky, The Bed that is a Tree

Second Prize: £200
   Sharon Black, Palomas

Third Prize: £100
   Claudia Jessop, Marionette Dream

Runners-up:

   Abegail Morley, Wasps

   Judith Taylor, Afterlife

   Will Johnson, a devotion

   Anna Wigley, Dear John

   Jane Lovell, The Prayer of St. Simon

Congratulations to the winners and runners-up. It was a tough competition. A line from a poem by Geoffrey Hill comes to mind: 'I would compose my voice'. Each of the winners and runners-up certainly do 'compose' their own unique voices and this is what makes their poems memorable.

John F Deane, in his enlightening book, *In Dogged Loyalty: The Religion of Poetry: The Poetry of Religion* (the columba press, 2006), states:

> If poetry is reduced to serving the needs of amusement, the loss to the human spirit is immense. Poetry pushes experiences that are inaccessible to rational disquisition; it works to lift the rationalist into the shocking position of dealing with things that go bump beyond the thin partition of human reasoning.

The poems chosen here all exert this special 'lift'. They also comply with

John F. Deane's definition of poetry as 'an instrument of disorder, but of a disorder that urges towards a finer, more humanity-serving, order'. Like all real poets, they aim for what Tom Paulin calls the creation of 'unhurried space for the unaccompanied human voice' (*The Secret Life of Poems, A Poetry Primer*, Faber and Faber, 2008).

Over a thousand poems were read carefully. Many were kept for special commendation, and notes written upon them to be sent back to the authors. Some poems were earmarked for future issues of *Agenda*, even though they were not the winners of the competition. It was interesting when all the poems were put back with their owners that the highlighted poems, though anonymous of course when read, nearly all belonged to familiar names that had appeared before in *Agenda*. There were many surprises and new poets to note, and some very accomplished poems, with assured, authentic voices that do deserve to get into print. It was felt, however, that the winning poems, and those of the runners-up (all a very close shave), had the edge over the rest. They seemed to have been pushed out of their writers, as if they had to be written. It was interesting to note, too, that by chance the three winning poets and the five runners-up are all published poets, and all women, with one exception. Also there was a good spread, with Scotland, Wales and England being represented in the prizes (not Ireland for once!).

A clutch of individual poems that were entered in the competition and link to the 'keening' theme of this issue have been chosen to be featured in the online supplement in tandem with this issue (along with paintings): www.agendapoetry.co.uk .

The worst entries were sentimental in a soppy way, used pat rhymes that bossed their authors, and archaisms such as 'thee', 'o'er', 'twixt', trying too hard to be 'poetic'. Others were like mere diary entries, with no interesting use of language and no music.

Kim Lasky's winning poem was picked out as the first prize-winner because of its potent mix of original, musical use of language, its clever distilling of the myth into a moving contemporary piece, with universal application, and because it mesmerised on the page and read like a spell.

Kim has a doctorate in Creative Writing and teaches at Sussex University and in various community settings. With the support of an Arts Council award, she is currently working on a collection of poems inspired by subjects as diverse as the theory of relativity and Glen Miller's *In the Mood*. Her work has appeared in various publications in the UK and US, and the pamphlet *What it Means to Fall* was published by Tall Lighthouse Press. Three sonnets by Kim, 'Kalypso' I, II, III, appeared in the 'Poems on Water' issue of *Agenda*, Vol 42, No 1, in 2006.

She says of her winning poem: 'I've long been fascinated by the *Odyssey*, not least because of the roles in the epic played by women who often act as the driving force behind events. Penelope's faithfulness to Odysseus and her cunning djin stalling the suitors by appearing to be weaving a shroud, which she unpicks each night, is often talked of by others but she speaks little herself. This poem imagines her perspective – one that might be more complicated than is usually told. The lament is an ancient Greek *threnos*, which would have been sung by mourners, interesting to me for its suggestion of the wire in the loom's reed and the night-time unravelling of Penelope's story.'

Sharon Black's 'Palomas' was a very close contender. It was marked out because it is such a successful public poem, and public poems are very hard to pull off. Again, this had an authentic ring, very movingly used Victor Zamora, the Chilean miner-poet for its persona, and conveyed brilliantly and imaginatively the plight of the trapped miners. The use of Spanish words and phrases in places made it all the more real.

Sharon, 42, is originally from Glasgow but now lives in the remote Cévennes mountains of southern France with her husband and their two young children. In her past life she worked as a journalist and as an English teacher in Japan and France. In France she runs a small retreat and organises creative writing holidays (www.abricreativewriting.com). Her poetry has been published in several anthologies and journals including *Mslexia, Envoi, Orbis, The Interpreter's House*. She won The Frogmore Prize, 2011, The New Writer competition 2010 for Best Poetry Collection and Envoi International Poetry Prize 2009. Her first poetry collection, *To Know Bedrock*, will be published by Pindrop Press later this year (www.sharonblack.co.uk).

Claudia Jessop's 'Marionette Dream' is a haunting lament about a loved person who has left. It cleverly uses the extended metaphor of the marionette, in a dream, in the first half. The second half is back in the harsh reality of coping with the loss of the person. As the poem is honed down to two last lines of single words, the emptiness that is emphasised echoes on after the poem's end.

Claudia has published poems in a number of magazines, and has been shortlisted in several competitions. Her first collection, *This is the Woman Who*, was published by Cinnamon Press in 2009. She lives in Hackney, where she has worked as an oral historian on local projects.

She says of her winning poem: 'It is a poem I had wrestled with for a long time and had nearly given up on several times, but I couldn't quite bring myself to abandon it, so it is really gratifying to feel that it had finally come together!'

The runners-up all wrote very moving, well-crafted poems in their own distinct voices that well deserved prizes, and could well have been in the top three. For the final choice, the poems were read aloud and chosen for their oral power as well, of course, for their authority on the page.

Abegail Morley is guest poetry editor at *The New Writer*. Her collection, *How to Pour Madness into a Teacup* was shortlisted for the Forward Prize Best First Collection; the title poem was previously nominated for the Best Single Poem. She was nominated for the London Best New Poet Award 2010 and has won or been placed in a number of competitions. Her work appears in a wide range of journals, including *The Financial Times* and *The Spectator*. Her work has also been widely anthologised, including in *Did I Tell You? 131 Poems for Children in Need* (2010). She lives in Cranbrook, Kent and teaches in Benenden School.

Judith Taylor comes from Perthshire and is now based in Aberdeen, where she works in IT. Her poetry has appeared in a number of magazines. Her first chapbook collection, *Earthlight*, was published by Koo Press (2006), and her second, *Local Colour*, by Calder Wood Press (2010). She has appeared at Shore Poets, StAnza, and at the Durham Book Festival, and is currently Managing Editor of *Pushing Out the Boat* magazine.

Will Johnson lives and works in Cardiff where he teaches Sanskrit and Indian religions at Cardiff University. Among his academic publications is a verse translation of Kalidasa's play, *The Recognition of Sakuntala* for Oxford World Classics. Now in his fifties, he started writing about ten years ago, and has previously published in magazines such as *Poetry Wales*, *Magma*, and *Envoi*.

Anna Wigley lives in Cardiff where she was born in 1962. She studied for a PhD on the novels of Iris Murdoch, then began publishing poetry and stories in the 1990s. She is now a freelance writer, having published four books with Gomer Press – three volumes of poetry and a collection of short stories. *The Bird Hospital* came out in 2002, followed by *Footprints* in 2004, *Dürer's Hare* in 2005, then *Waking in Winter* in 2009.

Jane Lovell lives in Rugby, Warwickshire and teaches at a nearby independent school. Her poems, which have been published in many journals such as *Poetry Wales*, *The New Welsh Review*, *Envoi* and *Myslexia* focus on man's relationship with nature. Threads of folklore and science run through her work.

Kim Lasky

The Bed that is a Tree

... and as she mourns him the tears run down from her eyes, since this is the right way for a wife when her husband is far and perished.
                                                                    The Odyssey Book XIV

Naked, I am without a sheet to wind me.

Even vacant sleep won't shroud me tonight;
so exposed, I notice the blood thinning
in my corpse-veins, hear the shrinking of skin,
see bare limbs decompose in the darkness.

Lost, a tragedy without a body.
Scraps of lament *my love I loved you well*
distract me in this bed that is a tree
where we should lie together *my love*

I kept you well (forgive my wanton grief)
like musk in the box and wire in the reed
in this bed that is a tree, where night falls
and things are not as they seem.

When night falls, the sea is a distant death.
Your bones roll in the wash of the breakers
and I hold the living near to me, saved.
My love I kept you well; this bed, this tree.

Easing wanton grief, they come to caress
my dreamless breast, but you come to me too;
the listing hull of a driftwood ship.
My love I loved you well; this tree, this bed.

So much done in darkness, unsaid. Night work
scorns the loom's reed, wires that would keep threads
apart are sidestepped. We come together
barbed in intimacy, secrets well-kept.

I look for you in them, my love, don't know
what they see in me. Aggrieved, perhaps
talons and beaks, the sharp flaunted freedom
of a woman always dreaming an eagle.

Lamenting: *like musk in the box, and wire.*

Sharon Black

Palomas

He ekes words from the colour of the soil,
from the reek of sixty days of urine, shit and sweat,
from his knowledge of each man's breath, the tension
at the earth's heart.

Written by the alchemy of rigged truck batteries
he tucks his letters, gently as eggs,
into the abdomens of white *palomas*:
news to hatch in his family's hands.

He tells how he's forgotten blue –
the wink of *el Salar de Llamara*;
the muscled flinch of swordfish;
a lone star, fading;

how he knows morning only from his wrist-watch,
from the 6am sudden stringed fluorescence,
from his daily ration
of half-a-spoon of tuna, one biscuit, a mouthful of milk.

He holds his notebook upside down
and lets the pages fall open like wings:
a pair for every man down here,
he must leave not one sheet empty.

Note: On 5 August 2010, 33 miners were trapped in the San José mine in Northern Chile. They survived for 69 days before being brought to the surface. Victor Zamora, a mechanic, sent up poems for his wife in plastic capsules nicknamed palomas ('doves'). The Chilean flag is known as la Estrella Solitaria ('the lone star').

Claudia Jessop

Marionette Dream

In a nightmare you appear
in the form of a puppet.

Straining to stand, tremble-tense on strings
held from above, head nodding to the side,
wooden feet and hands extend and twitch.

Someone has drilled holes
in sockets and joints, fed filaments through
to fistfuls of T-crossed slats,
to animate you
from above.

You slump and drape like a drunkard,
quiver to bobbing attention.
Your limbs clink, there's a carved smile
and carved stare, but I know it's you.

Then waking up, I see
your things still on your table.
Your writing things, loose leaves and spiral bindings,
propelling nibs,

and all the little faces
of watches, of lenses
of glasses, the circles you have left
of numbers,
and of light's gradations.

These inanimate things record you, I remember
you were not wooden, or hinged, or strung.
They let you take shape, breathing,
touched and touching,

four-chambered,
two-footed,
pulsing,
leaving.

Abegail Morley

Wasps

You left as I was washing my wounds with vinegar,
skin stinging, stuck full of pheromone –

it attracts violence you know, pheromone,
it yells to others *hit her, hit her, hit her.*

My eyes slip in their own liquid like wasps
skidding on sweetness in a jam jar trap.

By now you're 50 miles away at the Dartford Tunnel
thrumming your way through, while here my skull's stuffed

with wasps bashing their wings, wedged between
bone and skin. Soon their humming stops.

I see them sink in the syrup, their legs struggling,
compound eyes flicking mosaics, ocelli fuzzy,

out of focus. We look at each other for the first time:
my irises saffron, flaxen – sticky with sleep.

They drown as I tell them *he can't come back.*

Judith Taylor

Afterlife

Imagine this:
how Orpheus faked his own death
to be free of words, free of line, free
of the obligation
to have meanings or to dream of them
and came back

as a painter. Imagine
how attentively he grinds the colours, each one
uniquely indescribable.
How he hardly dares to whisper
even their names
for fear these words, too, betray him.

How he primes the ground.
How he loads the brush for the first touch
so tenderly, you imagine;
or with stuttering hands, rapacious
to begin again; and paints

 – what?
The dark lights he followed
under ground, and sees in his sleep yet?
The red and purple splatter of
beasts' viscera and old bones
he gave to wall-eyed madness?

Or the white sky
the yellow fields
the grey road in front of him

and the trees
that frame them, stark with angles,
shimmering with their own life.
Silver and brown and gold
and green and free of the obligation
to dance to anyone's song.

Will Johnson

a devotion

when I saw her at Jaipur
while the tyrant was napping
her feet barely shuffled the dust
it was like the end of a brush stroke
lifted in secret or a promise
still poised to go out

it was there that she made
me her scribe of ill omen
take what you need
from each trailed inflection
each knot and black feint
of my vagabond art

I fetched and refashioned
but her heart seemed to harden
from which they inferred
that before it was over
she'd banish my gaze
my licensed devotion
to the scullion end
of this desert house
that she'd die with my name
uncrushed in her mouth

they 'inferred' but were clueless
that rabble of mlecchas
who'd never seen mudras
distempered by moonlight
who were nowhere near Jaipur
when the tyrant was napping
the brush stroke ending
the future still wading out

and who knew nothing at all
of how I survived her
or how I'm survived by her art

Note: mlecchas – a Sanskrit term for 'barbarians' *mudras* – hand gestures

Anna Wigley

Dear John

Like a shipwrecked sailor you arrived that evening –
trembling in a sheen of sweat,
your rank shirt gaping to the waist.

We thought you were glad to be rescued
from the rotting life-raft of your home,
from the pee-soaked mattress and cruel floors
that punished you so hard for falling.

How could we know
that for the next three hundred days a single thought
would shake the shrivelled forest of your mind:
*'I must go now, it's getting late,
and this is not where I belong.'*

We locked you in a luxury cell
with rich food and clean linen,
with Sky TV and the symphonies of Brahms.
We told you it was right, we told you it was kind.

But daily, when you woke,
a stranger in a strange land,
you wanted only to return to that place
where everything was old and much-handled.

'I'm phoning the Police,' you told me once;
and who can blame you. I'd have called them myself
if I'd thought they could have helped –

helped you populate once more
that wrecked woodland in your head,
where only the oldest ashes and oaks remained.

Jane Lovell

The Prayer of St. Simon

I still smell the dust from the straw,
hear the squall of a broken cat hitting the feeder,
feel the crowd-roar slide away
as I thunder to the end of the gallops.

To be desecrated for my fame,
I had not imagined:
hooves severed and removed from below the knuckle,
hide slit with a steel blade, slippered off with bright knives
to be salted, scraped of skin and fat,
and reconstructed.

Here am I, encased upon a wall,
complete with creases, tufts,
the squiggle of a vein upon my lip,
ears angled to suggest high spirits,
blind.

My skeleton displayed for all to see
(arranged mid-gallop)
is now removed from view, dismantled to be stored,
ribs strung like fencing,
vertebrae aligned and numbered.

Without hooves, my legs taper like spines.
If I had my eyes, I would walk away on these spines,
skull soft wrapped like a macabre bride, grinning.

I would canter on my spines.
I would charge!
I would scatter the living like pigeons before a fox and climb the wind
with the sun slanting through my ribs,
striping the pitted turf,
flashing over the upturned faces of spectators,
streaming like silk through my bones.

Note:
St. Simon, the race horse, died from an apparent heart attack on April 2, 1908 shortly after his morning exercise at the age of 27. His hide was preserved and for some time was on display in a vertical wood and glass case in the entrance hall at Welbeck. His skeleton was given to the British Museum of Natural History at South Kensington, London, although it is no longer on display. A gold mounted hoof is on display at the Jockey Club in Newmarket, and another pair is in the Racing Museum at York.

Biographies

Timothy Adès is a translator-poet tending to use rhyme and metre, and widely published. His version of *Homer in Cuernavaca* by Alfonso Reyes won the TLS Premio Valle-Inclán Prize in 2001. Jean Cassou's *The Madness of Amadis* appeared from Agenda Editions in 2008. He translates Robert Desnos, Victor Hugo, Brecht and Sikelianós.

James Aitchison has published six collections of poems, the most recent being *Foraging: New and Selected Poems* (Worple Press). He is the author of the pioneering study of Edwin Muir, *The Golden Harvester*. His articles on creativity and poetics have appeared in *Agenda, Acumen, The Dark Horse, London Magazine, Montreal Review* and other journals.

Donald Avery was the librarian of a bioethics centre in London for over 20 years. Born in New Brunswick, Canada, he won the UNB Alumni prize for poetry at 16. He has written and recited since 1959, when Robert Frost advised: 'Keep the boy talking. One day he may have something to say.' Among those who have wished him a wider audience were John Betjeman and Kathleen Raine. His poem 'A Man of Letters' is included in the online supplement to the *Agenda* number in honour of Rilke, and 'The Final Page' in the Fiftieth Anniversary issue of *Agenda*.

Josephine Balmer's latest collection, *The Word for Sorrow*, was published by Salt in 2009. Previous collections and translations include *Chasing Catullus: Poems, Translations and Transgressions, Catullus: Poems of Love and Hate, Classical Women Poets* and *Sappho: Poems & Fragments*, all Bloodaxe. She is presently working on a study of classical translation and poetry for Oxford University Press's 'Classical Presences' series.

William Bedford is a poet, short-story writer and children's novelist, his work appearing in magazines around the world. His novel *Happiland* was shortlisted for the *Guardian* Fiction Prize and he has received Arts Council and Society of Authors awards for his poetry and fiction.

D W Brydon was born in Edinburgh in 1975. His poetry has also appeared in *The London Magazine* and previous issues of *Agenda*.

Kevin Cahill was born in Cork City, Ireland, in 1975, where he still lives. After graduating from University College, Cork with an honours degree in Government and Politics, he worked on European Commission projects in France. Returning to Ireland, he worked on the library staff at Cork Institute of Technology. He has also been a reiki practitioner. He is working towards a first collection of poetry and his poems have appeared in various UK and Irish journals such as *Magma, The SHOp, Orbis, Poetry Ireland Review, The London Magazine,* and *The Manchester Review*.

Belinda Cooke completed her PhD on Robert Lowell's interest in Osip Mandelstam in 1993. She has published three books to date: *Resting Place* (Flarestack Publishing, 2008); *Paths of the Beggarwoman: Selected Poems of Marina Tsvetaeva*, (Worple Press, 2008) and (in collaboration with Richard McKane) *Flags* by Boris Poplavsky, (Shearsman Press, 2009). She and Richard also have a collection of Boris Pasternak's later poems forthcoming.

Peter Dale's most recent publications are *Peter Dale in Conversation with Cynthia Haven*, published by Between the Lines Press, *Under the Breath*, poems, and *Wry-Blue Loves,* a verse translation of Tristan Corbière, which received a Poetry Book Society Recommendation for Translation – both published by Anvil Press Poetry, as is his terza rima translation of *The Divine Comedy*, now going into its seventh edition. His translation of Paul Valéry, *Charms and Other Pieces*, Anvil, appeared in 2007 and is now in its second edition. His current book of verse is the sequence *Local Habitation,* 2009, also from Anvil who will publish his new book, *Diffractions: New and Collected Poems* in 2011. He now lives in Cardiff.

Maureen Duffy is the author of 31 published works, including 6 collections of poetry, non-fiction, and 16 plays for stage, screen and radio, the most recent, being *Sappho Singing*. She is a fellow of the Royal Society of Literature and of King's College London, and a Vice President of the Royal Society of Literature, as well as President of Honour of the British Copyright Council and the ALCS, and a CISAC gold medallist. She was recently awarded a D. Litt by Loughborough University for contributions to literature and equality law reform.

Mary Fitzpatrick was last featured in *Agenda* in 2005. Since then, her poems have appeared in U.S. publications such as *The Dos Passos Review, ASKEW, The Georgetown Review*, and www.writersatwork.com Fitzpatrick, an organizational change manager in a large corporation near Los Angeles, holds degrees in writing from University of California and University of Massachusetts. The poems in this issue are part of a chapbook manuscript, *The Book of Leaving*.

Christopher Fletcher was educated at London and Edinburgh universities. His PhD focused on the aesthetics of British modernism and neo-romanticism, with one chapter devoted to David Jones. He was a curator of literary manuscripts at the British Library from 1995-2006, when he took up his present post as Keeper of Western Manuscripts at the Bodleian Library. He is a member of the English faculty in the University of Oxford and has published on a variety of professional and literary topics.

William Francis, 57, is a freelance editor and translator. He has lived in Normandy with his wife and three children for the last 12 years. Three or four years ago he started making collages, and is currently planning his third exhibition.

John Griffin lives in Ireland. He received his B.A. in Literature & Philosophy from St. Louis University, St. Louis, Missouri, and his MA and PhD from Washington University, St. Louis. He occasionally posts new writing and commentary at www.odradek-poetry. blogspot.com

Nigel Holt, 45, has lived and worked in the education field in the United Arab Emirates for a number of years. He has most recently been published in *Counterpunch*, *The Recusant* and *Snakeskin* magazines, and he has work forthcoming in many more journals, including *Poetry Salzburg*. He is editor of *The Shit Creek Review* (www.shitcreekreview.com)

Eleanor Hooker has been selected for the Poetry Ireland *Introductions Series 2011*. In April of this year she was awarded an MPhil in Creative Writing, with Distinction, from the Oscar Wilde Centre, School of English, Trinity College, Dublin. Her poems have been published in: *Agenda*, *Crannog*, *Wordlegs*, *The Stinging Fly* and *The SHOp* and in an anthology of new writing from the Oscar Wilde Centre, Trinity College Dublin, of the class 2009/10. Eleanor is a founding member and Vice-Chairperson of the Dromineer Literary Festival. She is a helm and Press Officer for the Lough Derg RNLI Lifeboat. Eleanor is working towards her first collection of poetry.

Robin Houghton's poems have appeared, and will appear, in *The Rialto*, *Iota*, *The North*, *South* and other journals. She is an internet marketer and copywriter by profession and lives in Lewes, near Brighton.

Gill McEvoy runs several regular poetry events in Chester (Zest!, The Poem Shed, Poem Catchers) . Two pamphlets of hers have been published: *Uncertain Days*, and *A Sampler* (HappenStance Press, 2006, 2008). A full collection. *The Plucking Shed*, came out from Cinnamon Press in 2010. Website: www.poemcatchers.com Blog: www.redbotinki.blogspot.com

Richard McKane is a poet and translator. He studied Russian and Classics at Marlborough College before going on to read Russian at Oxford. On graduation in 1969 his first translations of Anna Akhmatova came out from Penguin and OUP (a vastly expanded version was published by Bloodaxe in 1989). Thus started a long career as a poet and translator including books of Mandelstam (with Elizabeth McKane), Gumilyov, Olga Sedakova and Aronzon (to be republished and expanded by Waterloo Press in September 2011). He lived in Turkey for five years in the Seventies and co-translated, with Ruth Christie, Nazim Hikmet and Oktay Rifat. In 1978 he was awarded the Hodder Fellowship in the Humanities at Princeton. His most recent book of translations from the Russian is Larissa Miller's *Guests of Eternity* (Arc Press). His latest book of poetry, *Out of the Cold Blue, Poems 1999-1967* is published by Hearing Eye. He has written a long poem in Rubais: 'Trains of Thought' probably destined for the Internet. For sixteen years he worked as an interpreter of torture testimony at the Medical Foundation for the Care of Victims of Torture from Turkey and Russia before his retirement in 2005.

Stuart Medland, 57, has been a Primary School Teacher for most of his life. He has always written for the children he has taught and two small collections of poems for children *(Pine Cone* and *Harvest Mouse)* published locally are drawn from those years. Most of his writing is still inspired by natural history. An avid photographer of the wildlife of North Norfolk where he lives, he is also keenly interested by the way in which a photo may inspire or inform a piece of writing – or artwork.

His father, Lawrence Medland, died as a result of complications arising from prostate cancer eleven years ago. *Lol*, from which the poems in this issue of *Agenda* are taken, is part of a child's ongoing testimony to a fatherhood.

M.H. Miles lives and works in East Sussex.

W.S. Milne is a Scottish poet living in Surrey. His latest publication is a verse drama on Mary, Queen of Scots, printed in the magazine *Lallans*. His critical monograph, *An Introduction to Geoffrey Hill*, was published by Bellew (London) in 1998.

Lyn Moir has published collections with Arrowhead in 2001 and 2003. Calder Wood Press published *Easterly, Force 10* in 2009 and her fourth collection, *Velázquez's Riddle*, early in 2011. She lives in St. Andrews, on the harbour. She is working on a fifth collection.

Abegail Morley's collection *How to Pour Madness into a Teacup* was shortlisted for the Forward Prize Best First Collection (2011); the title poem was previously nominated for the Best Single Poem. She has been placed in competitions and won the Cinnamon Press Poetry Collection Award in 2008. She appears in various anthologies including *The Forward Book of Poetry (Faber), Did I Tell You (Children in Need)* and *The Sandhopper Lover* (Cinnamon), and also a wide range of journals including the *Financial Times, The Interpreter's House, Other Poetry* and *The Spectator*. She is guest poetry editor at *The New Writer*.

Tim Murdoch has taught yoga and practised Shiatsu treatment in the US and Canada. He now lives in Reigate. His poetry has been published in many magazines and journals such as *Acumen, Agenda, Pulsar, Smith's Knoll, South Bank Poetry* and *The Spectator*. He has performed at venues throughout the UK, US, Holland, Spain, and has contributed to poetry programmes for Radio Educación in Mexico City.

Jan Owen is a South Australian writer whose sixth book, *Poems 1980 – 2008*, was published by John Leonard Press in 2008. In October 2010 she was a guest at the Maastricht International Poetry Nights where *Der Kus*, a selection of her poems in Dutch was published by Azul Press. She is currently completing a manuscript of translations from Baudelaire's *Les Fleurs du Mal*.

Sergey Pantsirev was born in Moscow in 1969. He studied Computer Science at university, and has since been a free-lance journalist, and web designer. He has been writing poetry since he was 20 and his first book was published in 1994. The second volume of his poetry came out in 2004. He is also a translator. He is also CEO of an international software development company, and supports many prominent non-commercial internet projects in Russia. He is married, lives in Moscow and runs in international marathons.

Peter Rawlings grew up in London and New York and now lives in the South Pennines. Over the last two years his work has appeared widely in literary magazines.

Alonso Reyes 1889-1959 was a great Mexican man of letters: learned, versatile, a leader. He was an Ambassador in southern cities. His father, a general and Interior Minister, 'got himself killed in the Revolution'.

James Roberts is originally from Stoke-On-Trent but now lives in Hay-on-Wye where he writes about nature and place. His work as a dramatist has been produced in London. He has only recently begun writing poetry and his first pieces were published by The Dark Mountain Project. He currently works as a web editor.

Sue Roe is a poet, novelist and biographer who lives in Brighton. Her most recent books are *Gwen John : A Life* (Vintage) and *The Private Lives of the Impressionists* (Vintage), which has been translated into seven languages. Her book of poems, *The Spitfire Factory*, appeared in 1998 from Dale House Press. Her poetry is widely published in journals and anthologies including *New Poetries III* (Carcanet). She works with contemporary artists and has written exhibition catalogues for artists including Ellen Bell, Corinna Button, Marco Crivello and Anne Penman Sweet. She is a Senior Lecturer in Creative Studies at the University of Sussex.

Sarah Ruden was born in rural Ohio and educated at the University of Michigan, Harvard, and the Johns Hopkins Writing Seminars. She taught Latin and Greek literature at the University of Cape Town during the first years after the end of apartheid and won the South African Central News Agency Award for her collection of poetry, *Other Places*. She has since published four books of classical translation and *Paul among the People*, a study of the Pauline Epistles against their literary background. Translations of Apuleius' *The Golden Ass* and Aeschylus' *Oresteia* are forthcoming. She has been honoured with several anthology publications and prizes for poems published in magazines, and she held a Guggenheim fellowship in 2010-11.

Robert Smith was born in London, but has lived for several years in Cambridge where he works as a chartered secretary. A natural scientist by training but having a long-term obsession with poetry, especially poetry showing a hard edge, sharp imagery and controlled structure, he attempts the short forms in an effort to achieve an intensity of expression sought, with varying success, by the Imagists and with conspicuous success by certain French composers of the early twentieth century. He believes that the ideal poem should be austere and at the same time packed with evocative language.

Avril Staple studied Creative and Critical Writing at the University of Gloucestershire. She lives in Gloucester where she teaches creative writing and music.

Warren Stutely lives in Teddington. After studying composition, vocal technique and piano at The Guildhall School of Music, he was a specialist bookseller for 30 years until, more recently, his knowledge of early English music, art and culture led to his working at Hampton Court Palace. His main interests are English history, especially the early church, and modern/living British composers and painters, particularly the St. Ives School.

Marek Urbanowicz was born in 1953. He was Chairman of Brighton Poets in the late '90s. His work has been published in *Frogmore Papers*, *Weyfarers* and a current collection is in submission. He is particularly interested in the reading of poetry due to being the child of two actors and his own study of voice work. He has been qualified acupuncturist since 1979.

Dylan Willoughby had a limited edition, an illustrated poetry book, *Dusk at St. Mark's*, published by Chester Creek Press. The title poem and several other poems in the book appeared in *Agenda*. Willoughby has received fellowships from Yaddo and The MacDowell Colony (where he wrote 'Annwn').

Jackie Wills has published four collections of poetry. Her most recent is *Commandments* (Arc, 2007). She has been shortlisted for the T.S. Eliot prize and was one of *Mslexia* magazine's top ten new poets of the decade in 2004.